The sh*t
becoming a clinical
psychologist

READER ADVISORY

WARNING

**ONLY IF YOU DARE TO BECOME
A CLINICAL PSYCHOLOGIST**

By Dr Sarah Davies

About the author

Due to the controversial information documented throughout this book, the author wishes to remain anonymous and thus an alias name has been used to protect the author's identity. At the time of publishing this book, the author has and continues to practice as a clinical psychologist. The author works clinically in accordance to guidance and the Standards of Principles dictated by The Health and Care Professions Council, as well as policies and guidance dictated by NHS England, General Data Protection Regulation, The Information Commissioner's Office, and the British Psychological Society.

Disclaimer

The views shared in this book are not necessarily that shared by any professional establishment but are rather the personal thoughts and experiences of the author.

Acknowledgements

To my friends, family, and partner who supported me throughout this journey. You taught me I have two feet for a reason, to stand up tall and march to my own rhythm. You taught me to show kindness to myself when

I had nothing else. You taught me to be the best version of myself. For that I thank you.

Book Content

Preface

The journey of becoming a clinical psychologist is typically a very long, painful, and emotionally draining one. In fact, some people who go through this journey experience describe it as being quite traumatic. Given the level of psychological threat people undergo to get to the stage of qualifying as a clinical psychologist, yes, it can be traumatic. However, this is rarely spoken about, and definitely not voiced publicly. The horrors that people experience are usually kept secret due to fears of being punished as a consequence – because the punishment is real. The purpose of this book is to unveil the truth of what goes on behind the closed doors of becoming a clinical psychologist.

If you have ever met a clinical psychologist, more often than not they will be kind, patient, caring, thoughtful, full of smiles and empathy. All the good qualities that you can think of when imagining what a good clinician would be like and how they would help people. Generally speaking, most clinical psychologists are great clinicians and have the genuine desire to care for other people, which may have attracted them to this line of work in the first place. People wishing to become clinical psychologists usually have their heart in the right place, that they wish to create a better world for others, to improve other people's wellbeing, and do this with compassion and kindness. Unfortunately, the system surrounding how one becomes a clinical psychologist can be extremely harsh and punitive. The system embodies the very opposite qualities of how you envisage clinical psychologists to be. There is very little room for kindness or compassion. There is colossal room for criticism, threat, and maltreatment. People who become clinical psychologists rarely get to this stage of their career through encouragement and healthy growth where they feel nurtured, supported, and valued by their superiors including academic establishments. That would be wonderful, though is currently a distant reality. A more common reality is that people who become clinical psychologists are driven by fear and anxiety, with threat, pressure, and intimidation hanging over their head. Novices and people who have nothing to do with clinical psychology may not have necessarily noticed this. That's because it would be extremely dangerous for them to voice their concerns about the unsympathetic, unfair, and often callous treatment they experience throughout their professional journey. As in any abusive relationship, the abuser works tactfully as they hold all the power and control within the relationship, leaving the victim vulnerable to their will. The victim is powerless, doing what they have to do to survive, putting on make up to cover the bruising, and dancing like a puppet on cue with a smile on their face. Under that porcelain face of beauty and desirability is shattered glass. That is the reality of becoming a clinical psychologist. The system in which you have to follow to qualify as a psychologist holds all the control and power, which can be used to abuse you. You become helpless to the system, bowing down to its demands and following orders regimentally, suppressing instincts to liberate yourself. And similar to abusive relationships, you are taught to keep this all a secret, otherwise... who knows what punishment you will receive. Something worse than what you could imagine.

I am a clinical psychologist and I have worked clinically for several years. I have been tempted to write this book for quite some time; however, I was conflicted about doing so for such a long time. I was anxious about how I would be viewed by my colleagues, other clinical psychologists, and the field as a whole. I knew that although I have qualified and no one can take that away from me, I would get heavily criticised for even considering challenging the system which was created to train people to become clinical psychologists. You see, the criticism and the threat doesn't necessarily stop after qualifying. Clinical psychology is a small world and people know people. One person even makes a peep and the whole world seems to know about it. Or the people who are in control, at least. The entire aura around clinical psychology is that you should keep up that positive attitude, you should be grateful to have been given a chance to work towards becoming a clinical psychologist. Say a bad word and you risk losing it all – your reputation, your job, and your career.

The problem is that you would not only be criticised by superiors, people in power e.g. employers, supervisors, and academic institutions; you can also be criticised by your peers and other clinical psychologists. The reason why academic institutions would be critical of you is to maintain the status quo and power imbalance in that they remain all powerful, all controlling, and all demanding. Employers and supervisors would be unhappy with you as you would be giving off a negative vibe around your work, they would question how much you enjoy your work and whether you would be 'giving it your all'. Employers and supervisors understandably want someone who is driven and hardworking so that they are able to provide the best service to patients.

What I find most interesting is why your peers and other clinical psychologists would criticise you for speaking the truth about the pain you endured. I find reasons for this generally boil down to 4 things. (1) The individual may have submitted to the inequalities and power imbalances that they have become so worried they would be punished too by simply having an association with you. (2) They may have learned helplessness that the system will always be dominant and punitive, so why bother challenging it. (3) They may have an attitude that it is easier to just 'move on' by saying, "well yes getting to the stage where you finally qualify is a horrific process, but why complain about it now? You've got what you wanted, just work a 9–5 job and keep life simple". (4) They are actually a little deluded in that they believe that this is truly how the system should be, that it the system is justified in being harsh and punitive and we as minions are humbled by their grace and honoured to be considered good enough to work within the system. The fourth is the most worrying, as they will fight to honour the name of clinical psychology, believing they are doing all that is right, but sadly they too will be chewed out and thrown away by the system like the rest of us.

I have held myself back from writing this book which exposes the field because I was concerned that I would receive punishment. Like I said, even though I am qualified, there is the presence of threat if I challenge the power imbalance and status quo. The threat for anyone following qualification is losing their registration. For me, some people may view this book as me bringing the profession into disrepute, which could possibly lead to the loss of my registration. After much contemplation around what I would be risking by writing this book, I have decided that nothing will change if no one speaks up. Like any abusive relationship, the abuse will go on if the victim continues to succumb. Someone has to be honest and voice the real truth of what happens behind the scenes to change this problematic dynamic. I will not allow this abuse to continue. If my book only helps one person throughout their journey, I will consider it worthwhile. I have decided to take a stand to speak about real life experiences of the journey of becoming a clinical psychologist. This book will bring to light the injustices that occur in the field of clinical psychology, how people experience some forms of trauma throughout this process, as well as guidance around the steps you would have to take to succeed while preserving your personal wellbeing.

In order to protect myself and my vulnerabilities, I have anonymised elements of the book which would make me identifiable and I am operating under an alias name. I hope you understand that as much as I didn't want to do anonymise myself, I have had to take this step to preserve my welfare.

The purpose of this book

This book was written with the intention of helping people on their journey of becoming a clinical psychologist. Although there is information available through the internet, institutions, and books around career progression in this field, it is lacking in several areas: detail, accuracy, and the truth. Information out there talks about the general stages of one's career to becoming a qualified clinical psychologist: completing an undergraduate psychology degree, working as an assistant psychologist, and finally completing the clinical doctorate training programme. However, the information rarely reveals details of what each stage is like, the brutal challenges involved, and advice on how to navigate difficult situations. Little is documented on the agonising, derogatory, and deprecating experiences endured by most people who progress through this career journey. More often than not, the journey of becoming a clinical psychologist is portrayed as fun, involving significant levels of compassion and gratitude. No one speaks about the traumas that go on behind the scenes. That information is 100% censored. The positive image publicised around the career of a clinical psychologist is intentional. This is in order to appear 'aligned' with the values that are expected to be held by clinical psychologists. We often expect clinical psychologists to be kind, caring, and thoughtful (which most are); however people who go on to becoming a clinical psychologist rarely get treated this way during their career progression. Unfortunately, these people are usually treated with criticism, hostility, and oppression. Friends, that is the part that is kept secret from the public, and even people who are at their infancy of this career journey, as revealing such information would challenge the image of clinical psychology. People may go into denial, refusing to believe the truth as the truth is too uncomfortable. People who believe the truth may doubt those in the field of clinical psychology as the profession is brought into disrepute. In a way, it almost feels that a cult exists in that the honour of clinical psychology needs to be held, that this is the holy grail, and anything that questions or criticises the field needs to be exiled. This book questions that unhealthy, one-sided status quo by providing you a glimpse of the truth with detail and accuracy.

I have written this book from an autobiographical stance. As someone who has survived the traumatic career journey of becoming a clinical psychologist, I felt it was important to write this book from a personal perspective. To those of you reading, I have provided an honest narrative, telling you what it is really like so that you can understand the truth behind the masked field. Nothing is censored. With the honesty I provide, there will be information that may be hard to read as many experiences described are unpleasant and painful. This information is written to help others learn the truth behind this career and to help people who are going through this career path.

The chapters dictated in this book follow the general stages of this career in chronological order [undergraduate psychology degree, postgraduate Master's degree, assistant psychology posts, and the clinical doctorate training]. However, throughout the book I describe real experiences of pursuing the career of clinical psychology, the painful encounters, recommendations to succeed in both academic and clinical aspects of this career, as well as ways in which you maintain your wellbeing – because believe me, your own psychological wellbeing will be tested. Again and again. This book touches on the following areas:

- Academia:
  - The academic work involved within undergraduate degree, postgraduate degree, and clinical doctorate training.
  - Methods to effectively improve your learning and your academic performance in exams, assignments, and clinical doctoral research.

- Professional development:
  - Challenges within the professional environment including:
    - The workplace when faced with opposing, difficult, and unethical viewpoints.
    - Highly demanding workload and having unrealistic and unattainable expectations of its completion.

- Becoming a successful candidate for clinically relevant assistant psychologist jobs as well as the clinical doctorate training.
  - Ways in which to manage the above challenges and succeed.
  - Professional qualities that are desired in clinical psychologists as well as ways in which to develop desirable qualities.

- Interpersonal experiences:
  - Interactions with other people across different places including students, tutors, supervisors, assistant psychologists, and other professionals.
  - Challenges within certain interactions.
  - Ways to manage and navigate unhelpful interactions as well as attract helpful relationships.

- Personal wellbeing
  - Areas of this career that negatively impact one's personal physical health and psychological wellbeing.
  - Ways to preserve and prioritise one's wellbeing.

- Reflections for supervisors, clinical tutors, and clinical psychology training course providers:
  - Necessity of supporting the wellbeing of assistant psychologists and trainee clinical psychologists.
  - Supporting education for career development

Without further ado, I whisper to myself "good luck" as I tell you about the truth of this career journey.

CHAPTER 1
Let's talk: Psychology & mental health

"We are what we are because we have been what we have been, and what is needed for solving the problems of human life and motives is not moral estimates but more knowledge", Sigmund Freud. This statement epitomises humanity thus far as well as the need for constant pursuit of understanding of humanity. That's where the psychology comes in.

Psychology may be argued as the be all and end all of humanity. It is relevant to every single human and animal on this planet. As creatures, we all have lived and it is through life we experience a myriad of situations, interactions, physical ailments, hunger, threat, safety, success, failure, births, and deaths. As we move through life, our ultimate aim is to survive, to move away from and get rid of painful and threatening situations. We do whatever it takes to survive. We do what we believe works which is generally based on what we have experienced in the past that helped us survive. In this way, whether or not we consciously know it or even think about it, our life experiences become significant teachers as these guide our actions and behaviours in each situation we find ourselves in. Our experiences tell us what we should do in order to survive and remain as safe as possible. With this, our mind and brain become active as we calculate our chances of survival based on any given behaviour and thus we tend to choose the behaviour that results in the least amount of risk. This can even be seen going back to our Neanderthal ancestors who worked out how to survive by escaping dangerous animals, protecting themselves from harsh weather, obtaining food and water for sustenance, and creating communities for protection and reproduction. As any animal evolves with the progression of time and the fittest animal thrives, survival relies on genetics and the development of the brain, of which the two are interlinked, as well as one's behaviours to maintain safety. Although the argument differentiating the 'brain and the mind' continues in the world of research, there is a recognition that a relationship exists between the two, which involves one's thoughts, perceptions, memories, emotions, personality, and behaviours. As generations continue to survive, we become more and more aware of what will allow us to survive and thrive, and as humans we attempt to behave in line with such. In essence, this is the study of psychology.

In today's age, psychology of humans is used in almost all industries. There has been a growth in the study and application of human psychology with the aim of predicting the behaviours of people in certain situations and what drives their behaviours. Our personal psychology affects our personality, what we like and dislike, as well as our relationships with family, friends, and partners. We recognise that life events influence our belief systems, our values, and our behaviours which can also affect our emotions and thought processes. Businesses observe behaviours to identify the ideal advertising methods to become more appealing to customers. In the McDonalds 'M' symbol, the colour red is used to stimulate hunger and draw attention while the yellow promotes joy and friendliness. Employers use psychology to determine the type candidates who are most suitable for the job. Social media is used to elicit thoughts and feelings of desirability with respect to attractive qualities, physical appearance, as well as behaviours that are in line with social norms. Many physical illnesses can be alleviated with the power of the mind as seen with placebo effect and evidence from the field of epigenetics. Even the foreign exchange market trades trillions of US dollars daily based on human psychology more than the market itself. The list goes on and on. Psychology is literally all around us, regardless of the generation in which we live. Society as a whole has been able to progress by learning and understanding human psychology. To continue societal progression and the understanding of humans, the continued study of psychology is therefore necessary.

The field of psychology has expanded in which more and more people are showing an interest. Societies have become increasingly aware of how we as human beings respond to particular situations we face. We have developed more of an understanding around how situations influence images and thoughts we develop in our minds as well as our emotional responses and how we behave as a consequence. For instance, when inspired by the prospect of success, we may have positive thoughts that we are intelligent and we are leaders, we may feel joy, and we may engage in behaviours that we believe will help us succeed. If on the other hand we experienced a negative experience such as a relationship breakdown, we may feel heartbroken, we might experience images in our minds of their future absence, and we might grieve our sorrow or distract ourselves from the heartache. These are just examples of situations that we commonly experience or witness someone else experience. In all truth, every situation we experience in our every day to day life affects our mental, emotional and behavioural responses. We might feel sad if we are sick and stay in bed, we might feel happy if we are loved and look after ourselves better, we might feel scared if we are intimidated and run away or implement security measures, we might feel angry if we have been wronged and fight for justice, we might feel guilty if we saddened someone and try to correct it, or we might feel disgusted at certain situations so we avoid these. Irrespective of what we have lived through, as human beings we have all experienced some form of mental, emotional, and behavioural response, ultimately shaping our mental health. As our physical health is made up of matter, our mental health is made up of our thoughts, emotions, and behaviours. Our mental health involves our psychological wellbeing, and the more we know about our psychological wellbeing, the better equipped we are to promoting positive mental health.

We may not always be aware of our emotional and mental responses to situations we live through. Previous generations may have paid less attention to these, together with mental health, but this does not mean that emotional responses and mental health did not exist. As time has gone on and each generation attempts to do better than the last, we have allowed ourselves to pay more attention to our emotional responses and our mental health. Reading this, you may be familiar with the ongoing stigma around mental health difficulties as well as the battle to increase awareness and acceptance of these. Similar to physical health in that the human body requires inputs like oxygen, healthy foods, and exercise; so too does mental health require affection, compassion, and understanding to promote nourishment and growth. Like in physical health, the absence of care and the neglect of our health can lead to problems; so too does the neglect of our emotional and psychological needs lead to mental health problems. They say knowledge is power, and if this is the case, then the more we permit ourselves to understand and promote knowledge around human psychology, our emotional, mental, and behavioural responses, the more society that becomes able to accept mental health. It is the recognition of mental health problems as well as the desire to study and improve it that led to the field of clinical psychology and psychiatry. Given that psychiatry is beyond the remit of this book, we will solely be focusing on clinical psychology.

So, what about you?

If you have picked up this book, chances are you were drawn to clinical psychology for some specific reason. It may have been that you were interested to understand people, why people act in certain ways, what emotions and thoughts are driving their behaviour, and how you could support their mental health. A part of you may have wanted to understand yourself better, recognising that you have experienced emotional and mental turmoil at some point in your life. You may have wished to learn how to protect and promote your psychological wellbeing in order to have a more emotionally satisfying life. You may have had family members or friends who have struggled with their emotional and mental responses, behaving in challenging ways, which left you wanting to understand and support them. Some of you may be very clear about your reasons for being attracted to the field of clinical psychology. For others, reasons may be ambiguous but chances are, it will relate to you in some way. Like I said before, whether or not we know it, we have all experienced emotional, mental, and behavioural responses to every situation in life. Before we delve further into this book, it would be helpful for you to consider the forces driving your desire to study clinical psychology. Becoming more aware of this may help you become a clinical psychologist, making you a better student, teacher, and clinician.

Throughout this book, we talk about the journey you will embark upon in order to become a clinical psychologist. There are various different stages that you will go through as you develop your career in this field and with each stage you will face opportunities as well as challenges. Similar to that I talked about earlier, there will be situations you will face during your journey that absolutely affect your emotions and mental processes. If I may be completely honest now, not all of these situations will be 'good' and many will feel uncomfortable, challenging your own mental health. However, you will learn, grow, and develop as a human being from experiencing the different stages of this career. And if you don't learn or develop the ability to reflect upon yourself or your actions, which by the way many people do not, I can guarantee you will fail in this line of work. This book is designed to give you the full truth about what it takes to become a clinical psychologist, the situations you will face, the types of problems and challenges you will experience, how to self-reflect, factors that will help you develop professionally, and how to support your personal psychological wellbeing and mental health throughout this process.

As much as this book describes the professional journey of clinical psychology, you will also be going on a personal journey as you work your way to becoming a clinical psychologist. You will change as a person. The person who you will be when you qualify as a clinical psychologist will definitely be different than the person who started the journey. With each experience you have, your emotional, mental, and behavioural responses will change. Your thoughts, beliefs, attitudes, values, and personal psychology will change. "[You will] meet yourself time and again in a thousand disguises on the path of life", Carl G. Jung.

CHAPTER 2
The 'basic' career path

"No matter how big the lie, repeat it often enough and the masses will regard it as the truth", John F. Kennedy.

What they tell you to do in order to become a clinical psychologist: do a degree in psychology, maybe a Master's degree, work as an assistant psychologist for a year or two, and then apply for the clinical doctorate training programme. Three years later and voila, you are a clinical psychologist. Sounds straightforward, right? For anyone who has tried becoming a clinical psychologist you will know that the path may not be as easy or as simple as described. If anything, pursuing this career can almost feel like you are repeatedly being punched in the face, beaten up black and blue. The 'simplicity' indicated around the stages of this career can be deceiving, and the level of deception is only known to those who dig deeper on their path to becoming a clinical psychologist.

The purpose of this book is to tell it like it is. The honest experiences and reflections of a clinical psychologist who 'made it'. As a side note, if you wish to remain in denial or want information to be provided in a gentle way, put this book down and burn it, or if you are listening to the audiobook version, just stop right here. This book is unsuitable for you. You might find the information too brash or harsh, and you would be right, there are times when I do speak a little bluntly about the experiences that you will face. For you folk, I recommend you look into information and materials on Google or Amazon that are a bit softer to read, books that supposedly 'guide' you. Although such literature may be nicer to read, I guarantee you will be missing a lot of vital information that tells you exactly what to expect from this career journey as well as what will help you gain a better chance of success. The information you find online or described by universities is vague and obscure, leaving you lost and alone to find your own way. Avoiding the reality of this career and sticking with the romanticised story talked about by the institutions or professionals representing institutions, you would ultimately be doing yourself a disservice. You would be neglecting your need to know the full picture of how to become a clinical psychologist, the challenges you will face personally and professionally, and how to manage and overcome these challenges. If you are willing and wanting to know the harsh reality of what it takes and what goes on behind the scenes, this book tells it like it is. I must be clear, I have not and will not filter anything. I am taking a personal risk in being so honest with you but this is my truth, naked and vulnerable.

Throughout this book, there will be some negative comments which may be hard to read at times. I don't want to put people off this career but I feel like it is my responsibility and moral obligation to be transparent about what it involves because, like I said earlier, much of the information out there on the internet or at universities is superficial, ambiguous, and sometimes just plane false. Many of the other clinical psychologists I have come across do not talk about the heartache, anguish, and potential 'trauma' that comes along with pursuing this career. They do not talk about this as it would be viewed as 'taboo', fearing punishment by the All Mighty Health and Care Professions Council (HCPC) for even hinting the profession into disrepute. How dare you think a single critical thought that might tarnish the profession. Don't you know? Clinical psychology is the beacon of hope, shining light that breaks through the clouds of all other professions and is clearly the righteous choice of all mental health care professions. The aura surrounding clinical psychology almost forces you to hail the profession and be constantly positive about it, even if it is absolute BS. If anything, people say you should count yourself lucky succeeding as a clinical psychologist. They say things like "be grateful, don't complain, work hard, work even harder", eventually leading to the normalisation of self-sacrifice because you are doing it for the greater good (whatever that might be). Blood, sweat, and tears are certainly involved at various points. I can honestly say it is one of the most challenging career paths I have come across. I know I have not pursued all careers out there; however, I have broached a couple – including accountancy and dentistry – and I can say they seemed easier to penetrate than this one. Meeting other people from different professions, there has been a general consensus that becoming a clinical psychologist is certainly not easy. I'm not saying it is all bad, but there are some definite challenges.

For starters, I just thought it might be helpful to label potential initial questions you might have about me. Firstly, you might be asking yourself, why am I even talking about myself? I am sharing my personal experiences as these experiences are real and they are common among many people in this profession. These personal narratives are intended to help you understand the true experiences of one's journey to becoming a clinical psychologist. Furthermore, given this career is about helping and caring for others, I talk about my experiences to help you through this journey and provide wisdom so you do not struggle alone like I did. I talk about what a tyrant this career can be, the challenges you are likely to face, and how to manage these obstacles to succeed. Another question you might be asking yourself, "why is this author so negative?". And with that, you might also be saying to yourself, "the author is just one person, she might have found it hard but that won't happen to me, I'm determined and this is something I really want. I have all the right qualities and I will do it!". Well, that may well be true. You are different to me and your approach to this career journey may be different. However, chances are you picked up this book because there is a niggling sense of uncertainty or unclarity around the career: How do I get into it? What can I do to become successful? Why does this feel like a constant uphill battle? Is it worth all the effort? And what are my chances? If you Google 'how to become a clinical psychologist', you will get hundreds of thousands of hits. A lot of this information will essentially tell you what I mentioned at the start of this chapter: go to university, become an assistant psychologist, complete your doctorate in clinical psychology training. This may be true to an extent; however, there is little around the real lived experiences of what this actually involves: what helps, what doesn't help, what will support your growth and development, and what will destroy you. Yes I did say destroy – which I mean both professionally and personally. This book gives you that insider information.

Now we come to the other side of the web, the source of all modern day knowledge. This is the side that leads you to psychology forums, claiming to create a 'helpful community' filled with 'useful information' in guiding you to become a clinical psychologist. On these sites you will find people at various stages of their career; students, assistant psychologists, or nursing assistants, talking about trying to crack their way into clinical psychology. If you have reached one of these sites, please delete the site from your history search, block the site, and step away from your laptop or mobile phone. These forums can be extremely toxic and damaging for your own psychological wellbeing and esteem. You may begin to notice how much people complain about the problems they faced, the numerous times they applied to the clinical doctorate training course and didn't get an interview, or making others jealous by showing off their success. People addicted to these sites, either writers or just standby spectators, will fall into the pit of doom. Many people accessing these sites are feeling anxious, fearful, and threatened that their life will come crashing down as a result of pursuing this career due to its competitive nature and instability. These people are in a lot of emotional pain and distress which is incredibly difficult for them. They are essentially wanting to seek help and reassurance from 'anyone who is listening', but unfortunately that includes no one on these sites. Some spectators of the doomsday parade may absorb some of this fear and fall apart while other's ego may grow so big they need to move to outer space as they watch those who struggle. As said by Lou Holtz, "[when telling people your problems], 20% don't care and the other 80% are glad you have them". This encompasses the reality of these psychology forums. So please, for you guys who are struggling, back away from these sites, they will not help you. And for you guys thriving off these sites, please give your head a little pin prick so you can come back down to reality. Healthy and successful growth (for both your career and personal wellbeing) cannot come from a place where such threat exist. Every individual has their own personality, worries, emotions, attitudes, and career journeys. One person's experiences does not take away anything from another and vice versa. So please, if you have struggled and come across such sites, step back and speak to someone who has the capacity and ability to help.

This book is designed to provide useful information from lived experiences without fuelling toxicity. From someone who has been there, done it, and progressed through the NHS banding and has her own private practice, I want to give you the best insights into what it takes and how to get there. I hope that after reading this book, you can make your own decisions and own reflections on your path and journey for your career and more importantly, for your life.

Just to give you an idea of my journey, here is a quick description of my CV:

- Undergraduate degree, BSc (Hons) in Psychology, graduating with a 2:1; 3 years
- Master's degree, MSc in Clinical Psychology, graduating with a Merit; 1 year
- Assistant psychologist working on research trials, inpatient mental health units, and high secure prisons; 3 years
- Temporary work as a nursing assistant and telephone counsellor; 3 years
- Clinical doctorate training; 3 years
- Clinical psychologist working across inpatient mental health settings
- Clinical psychologist developing and working in private practice
- Conducting and publishing research projects throughout my career

As outlined in 'The purpose of this book', I share details of what it is like to pursue this career, discussing the different academic and professional stages, the highs and the lows, and the challenges you will face. I describe what would and would not help you professionally to progress in this line of work as well as what will help you maintain your personal wellbeing while you are on this career journey. As I discuss a breadth of topics, the tone of my writing alters from sharing my personal experiences, providing informative knowledge to giving self-help guidance. This is to help readers develop wisdom related to their professional development as well as experience validation of their emotional pain during this difficult journey and gain permission to show themselves compassion. There will be times when I show a bit more of my 'honest brutality' which may come across as comical, but I assure you, all of my words come from a place of sincerity and the desire to help and support you. I also use the terms 'patients' and 'service users' interchangeably throughout this book to refer to people who receive care from services. I hope that this book allows you to recognise that while the path of becoming a clinical psychologist is difficult for anyone who attempts to walk it, the need for determination, self-belief, and self-kindness are necessary for success.

Principle 1:

"Life is not easy for any of us. But what of that? We must have perseverance and above all confidence in ourselves. We must believe that we are gifted for something that this thing must be attained", Marie Curie.

CHAPTER 3
First things first: Get learning

Undergraduate psychology. What is the point again?

University, a time to prosper, to learn, to grow, and to develop. You've sobered up from the drunken night out last night, you've got blisters on your feet, perhaps you have no idea whose apartment you've ended up in, and you realise you smell of greasy pizza. Go home and get a shower, retain a sense of dignity before it gets flushed down the toilet. Ah, now you are ready to go to your lecture, do your assignment, or perhaps just clean out the mess in your living room. I know for me, chances are I was doing the latter in an attempt to avoid work. I suspect it might be the same for many of you too. I guess this begs the question: why are we avoiding such work or being productive? What is driving the procrastination? Often, we might procrastinate because we do not feel inspired or motivated by whatever it is that we 'should be' working towards. We might want to want to study, but in all honest truth we just find it plain old boring. Alternatively, we might find that work too difficult, it might be overwhelming and too intimidating for us to start. A small part of us might be worried that we will fail and therefore if we do not try, we cannot fail. The problem with all of this is that we might end up in a place where we feel paralysed, demotivated, and the work remains incomplete. That can be scary when the deadline feels close. The good news is that many people do experience this, you are not alone. So please, sober up, eat something good, have a shower, and let's begin.

First of all, why did you do psychology as an undergraduate degree? Was it an interest in the field? And if so, what specifically about it fascinates you? Do the lecturers actually discuss these areas? Unfortunately, more often than not what is taught in lectures feels quite abstract and is in fact irrelevant to real life situations. It is distant from what we want to know or what excites us. To be fair, psychology is so broad and involves so many subjects, so it makes sense that many of these may not particularly interest us. For example, I remember one of my lectures relating to visuo-spatial skills which I found so unbelievably dull. Looking back now, I am unsure whether that was because of the subject itself or whether it was the monotone voice and grey appearance of the lecturer. Either way, I could not get into the subject. I recall struggling to complete an assignment around this subject or even revise for the exams. I'm sure that many other people experienced similar issues where they may not enjoy certain areas and it feels like such a drag to study. Other than this experience teaching me the importance of being an engaging lecturer, I also learnt that such subjects are difficult to engage with because it feels pointless. By that I mean, where is the real-life application? All that we learn in psychology should be applied to real life. That is the whole purpose of psychology: it is the study of human beings. Therefore, we should always understand how this theoretical subject translates to real life. When we understand this and when we identify how this can affect us, how we can observe this, and how we can enhance certain situations to our advantage, that is the real exciting part. When we get to the stage, we feel motivated to learn and to understand more, thus our comprehension grows and our competency increases.

Now, looking back as a qualified clinical psychologist, I see the usefulness of examining and understanding visuospatial cognitive skills. I have seen service users with brain injuries and disabilities that might struggle with such areas and therefore require support for example, when trying to cross the road. Knowing more about this helps me and such people to identify their difficulties as well as compensation strategies. The real life application is crucial in order to help people survive and thrive. This is different to learning about how shapes move and our eyes play tricks on us – like why the red and black spinney sign at the barbers is not actually spinning, or that dot you should stare at and all of a sudden your life changes as Jesus appears right before your very eyes. As interesting as this might be, I struggle to see its practical relevance other than showing it to my friends for 2 minutes of amusement. I found it is easy to largely ignore such topics and I avoided studying it when I could, actively swerving any learning as I found a comfortable position to take a daytime nap. With such topics, I literally gave it the minimum amount of time necessary because I simply did not find it worthy (wow I sound entitled, for shame). I would 'parrot learn' this topic just to pass the exam and quickly forget all about it as soon as time was up. Not that it really matters now because I've compensated for my past laziness, but I wish I paid more attention as this could have supported my clinical work if I considered its practical application and how it actually helps people. Unfortunately, I did not have a lecturer to guide me in such a way of thinking. I suspect that the task of the lecturer at the time was to get students to pass the exams, thus teaching the module textbook style.

"In school you're taught a lesson and then given a test. In life, you're given a test that teaches you a lesson", Tom Bodett. "Education...has produced a vast population able to read but unable to distinguish what is worth reading", George M. Trevelyan. "Education is learning to grow, learning what to grow toward, learning what is good and bad, learning what is desirable and undesirable, learning what to choose and what not to choose", Abraham Maslow. "Education is not the learning of facts, but the training of the mind to think", Albert Einstein. The problem with university is that the lecturers often teach you to pass the exams or assignments, they rarely ever teach you to learn, how you should learn, or what are the relevant real-life applications. There is a significant difference between being the recipient of schooling and actually learning about a subject. As a student, you can parrot rehearse the subject to pass exams but fail to actually learn anything useful. As much as you have received schooling at a higher education, but you have not learnt anything. You can rehearse studies along with names and dates as well as theoretical ideology. You might do well in a pub quiz. How about the pub quiz of life? Learning involves actual understanding of the topic and its implications. Bad teachers (unfortunately there are a lot of them), will help you pass the exams but it is up to you to choose whether you simply attend university for the piece of paper at the end or learn something that affects the future clinician in you.

In order to successfully learn about such subjects, we need to first learn and develop the skill of thinking; we must be able to think independently and creatively in order to become knowledgeable and develop as individuals, academics, and professionals. Let me ask you this, have you been told you must study a particular subject, and it felt completely useless? This might remind you of school days where Mr Moustache said, "you must learn trigonometry otherwise you will fail in life". Oh yes, I forgot that right angles put food on the table, silly me. During your psychology degree, chances are you have experienced times when the subject felt purposeless. This is perhaps because its current real-life application seemed vague and you were given a bunch of names, dates, and figures to learn. My hunch is that like me, you were not taught how to think, you were taught how to regurgitate information. To make your time at university worthwhile and increase your likelihood of success, it is important that you learn how to think, and knowing how to think will help you learn further. Unfortunately, learning how to think has been a skill somewhat missed across much of educational institutions, from school all the way up to higher level education.

Rather than simply aspiring to be the next Alex, the African Grey parrot, developing the skill of thinking and learning means we need to consider two main areas: the first relates to our motivation to think and learn, and the second relates to how we go about learning. Dealing with the first issue, I have noted questions below that can help you reflect upon the importance of the subject. Considering these questions can help you think about the purpose of the subject and guide you to topic areas that would be important for you to think about and learn. In other words, you begin to think about what is important, what it is you should learn, and why it is you should learn this. Thinking of these questions enhance your openness and motivation to think creatively and learn independently. These questions can be used at any point when approaching education:

- Why did the first pioneers begin exploring this area?
- What do we know about it so far?
- What was the context (environmentally, socially, relationally etc.) when this area was initially explored? What is its current context?
- What do we need to find out about it, but is currently unknown?
- How would this subject be useful to myself and / or other people?
- How could this information improve humanity?
- What would have to happen for this subject to become more beneficial to myself / other people / society?
- Would you want to implement the teachings of this subject? How could you? And why would you (or why would you not)?

When approaching a subject, it is important to consider its relevance to humans and its real life application. If we do not consider these questions, we are simply learning for the sake of 'getting a degree' and it goes no further for ourselves, our career, or the science of psychology. If we consider the above questions, we can begin to relate to topics such as cognitive psychology, relationships, self and social identity, and we can understand their importance. Holding these questions in mind, we can become skilled in the art of thinking, seeking out materials that are useful and relevant to learn. Considering these questions we can develop the desire to think deeper about the subject and become more motivated to learn.

The questions above will allow you to begin thinking about the specifics of the subject areas that are important and relevant for you to learn. To further support your thinking and learning, I have included questions below which may allow you to consider methods in which you would go about learning.

- How confident am I that I can learn about this subject? (and record this on a scale of 1-10; 10 being the highest score)
- What has led me to this score?
- What would have to happen to improve my score and make me more confident?
- In other areas, university subjects or otherwise, what am I knowledgeable in? How did I develop this knowledge? Why did this help me develop knowledge?
- What methods have I used to learn about the subject? How well did it work? What did I miss? Is there a way of improving how I learnt?

Considering these questions can help develop confidence to learn further about a particular subject. You consider ways in which you have successfully learnt about something in the past as well as how you can do this again to enhance your knowledge. These questions will help you identify your learning style. If you are unsure of your learning style, try thinking of any subject (not necessarily related to psychology) that you know a lot about or that you learnt about. Examples may be about animals, playing an instrument, hair styling, make-up application etc.. Now consider, how did you come to develop such knowledge or skill? Was it through physical practice, watching videos and tutorials, reading about it, speaking to others about it? Neil Flemming's VARK model discusses different learning styles. If you want, you can complete the VARK Questionnaire version 8. at https://vark-learn.com/the-vark-questionnaire/ to help you identify your own learning style. Considering the above questions as well as your learning style, this may support the actions you take in order to think and learn about the subject to the best of your abilities.

Developing the skills to think and learn as well as enhancing motivation and confidence to do so is vital to support your career progression; to perform well during university and beyond academia. This book does not have space to discuss the methods of thinking and learning in further detail, nor is it the purpose of the book; however, I urge you to consider the difference between attending university and learning, while having the wisdom to choose how you approach education. It is crucial to make the process of learning meaningful so that we can become the best version of ourselves – both professionally and personally. Specifically related to your psychology degree, it is such a broad umbrella and naturally you will be drawn to certain topics more than others. However, it is important to recognise the relevance of the topics we are required to study as well as how we would develop knowledge about these topics in order to become successful academics. This can in itself be one of the first steps to making you a better prepared to becoming a clinical psychologist.

Principle 2:

In order to learn what is needed, it is necessary to learn how to think, consider why this subject is important, how is it meaningful, and how it impacts humanity.

CHAPTER 4
Graduating with a good grade

I don't know what you heard, but I was always told by clinical psychologists as well as lecturers that it was imperative to graduate with a 1st class grade in order to have a shot of becoming a clinical psychologist. I remember working so hard in the hope I would achieve that grade. As much as I went out and partied in my first year of university, I frequently declined nights out or socialising with friends in the second and third year because I felt my time should be focused on studying. I woke up early every morning between 5:00 and 6:00 AM and I would go to bed around midnight. I would spend most of the days in the library studying, reading reams and reams of research, revising for exams, and repeatedly going over assignments that were due to be handed in. The university library I went to was weirdly open 24 hours a day, seven days a week. This was perhaps an unhealthy thing for someone like me at the time. I often used to take advantage of this world that never sleeps, particularly when I was anxious about the quality of my work or upcoming exams. I recall a time in my third year of university when I stayed in the library till about 3:00 in the morning and then decided to walk home because I was hungry and none of the nearby supermarkets were open. If there had been an open supermarket, I probably I would have gone back to the library and decided that the library was a great place to live. As you could imagine my physical health went out the window. My sleeping pattern became erratic and / or I was sleep deprived. My eating habits were appalling as I ate those cheap meal deals. I barely moved more than 300 steps a day as I would only move away from the computer to go to the bathroom then plop back onto my seat. I probably aged around 31 years living this lifestyle; 19 going on 50. Attractive. Certainly, this would not have been good for my arteries nor would it have been good for my brain. I also lost friends during the time, not that I necessarily ignored them; however, I absolutely let my personal relationships suffer as I did not feel that they were as important as my studies.

This was clearly one of those moments in my life where I sacrificed my personal physical and mental wellbeing in the attempt to work towards my career, even at such an early stage. I became so obsessive believing that it was crucial that I graduate with 1st class honours so that any employer would even consider looking at my job application. I believed that I would never get an assistant psychologist position if I did not graduate with a 1st class degree. Therefore, the sacrifice of my personal immediate needs felt justified for the hope of a better future and ultimately career. The voice of one clinical psychologist I came across always stuck in my mind, eating away at me, "if you don't get a 1st, unfortunately you are not going to be much of anything". In my mind this translated to "if you are not the best, you have failed in life and you may as well be a toilet brush". What an awful thought to have and what an awful message to be delivering to someone. I would often look around me and see my peers who were so intelligent, and I just felt incredibly inadequate in comparison. I frequently thought that I could never compete with them. I felt like the dumb person in the class and I had to work extra hard just to catch up to everyone else's level. This compounded the idea that it was acceptable, if not necessary, to sacrifice and neglect my personal wellbeing in order to become something more than an item that sh*t would cling to.

The very nature of clinical psychology as a career is highly competitive. This is often reflected in the characteristics of people who approach this career. These are people who have exceptional standards of themselves, striving for perfection, and fearing rejection and / or failure. Such people may experience critical voices inside their head which tell them they are not good enough and they need to continue working harder as perfection is moving further away. They may be more willing to sacrifice parts of themselves in order to become good enough or to meet their goals and desires. Not only are they likely to experience difficult emotions, but their wellbeing is also negatively impacted as they self-sacrifice and self-neglect.

I would have to say I was one of these people. I always believed I was not good enough and therefore would have to work harder compared with other people. In addition, receiving the message that I would have to graduate with a 1st class honours degree did not help as this magnified the pressure that I was under. I can imagine many people being in similar positions. They might be anxious about their own abilities and therefore study and revise for months on end, do extra reading, and repeatedly go over their work in the hope that this work will pay off. Of course, studying more does tend to mean you are more likely to get better grades. However, where is that line that determines how much is good enough before negatively impacting your wellbeing. One time during my third year, I was in the library and I began to have a panic attack thinking about the prospect that I might not graduate with a 1st class honours and therefore I was as good as the gum stuck at the bottom of your shoe. I fretted about getting this grade and I did everything I thought I could do to make that happen, but somehow whatever I did was never enough and I could never be good enough. When I noticed that it became harder to breathe and my body was filled with tension and panic, I went into a quiet corridor, fell to the floor, and cried. I must have been crying for at least 45 minutes. It felt as though my life came crashing down and I had no prospect or hope of making anything of myself. Such doom came upon me. Getting to this stage was a clear sign that my wellbeing was horrifically impacted. I crossed that fine line a long time ago that I could no longer see it on the horizon. My mental wellbeing also heavily affected in that I was unable to recognise what was a healthy and reasonable amount of work. In addition to the sleepless nights and poor health choices, I am sure my cognitive abilities declined. I couldn't think straight. I struggled to problem solve. I could not absorb the information that I was reading when studying. At this stage, studying more definitely did not mean becoming 'good enough'.

This experience taught me there is a limit to what is healthy for your personal wellbeing as well as your career progression. Be mindful and aware of what is healthy and what is not. If you are one of these people who has a negative story in your mind, or you have negative beliefs about yourself and your abilities, studying more might not necessarily guarantee better success. If anything, over-studying may hinder your success. It would be more important to work on the narrative inside your head, figure out how this can be shifted so that you can show compassion and care for yourself as well as maintain a level of healthy psychological wellness. My story is a classic example of how my basic needs were not met. Plainly, I denied myself of my basic needs. Even reflecting on Maslow's hierarchy of needs, I was not allowing myself to have a healthy foundation for my pyramid of needs. I did not allow myself to sleep fully or eat properly, two important components of basic human needs. What else was I to expect but everything else to come collapsing down? If my foundation was not solid, I would never be able to build up to become a better version of myself, to achieve my full potential. I needed to sleep and eat but I even felt it was acceptable to sacrifice these. It even tipped over to me believing that it was ok if I did not sleep or eat because I hadn't worked hard enough to deserve these things yet; being denied these needs almost felt justified. It meant I would have to continue working without eating or sleeping until it felt like I had done enough, which by the way never felt enough. What was all of this sacrifice for? Nothing. My head was so fogged up, none of my studying went in anyway. I didn't understand what I was studying by the end of it all. So please think about your basic needs, think about how you can fulfil these in a healthy way. Think about why it is important to meet your own needs, and if you don't, neither will your tutors and lecturers. Meeting your basic needs is the only way to stabilise that foundation so that you are able to move upwards and progress to the best version of yourself. Thus, you would be both accomplishing positive wellbeing and improving your knowledge, setting you up for the right path.

Getting back to the idea of graduating with a 1st class honours – although this would be nice, I can say this is not a necessary requirement. I achieved a 2.1 and I was able to progress in this career. As a qualified clinical psychologist, many people I interviewed were appointable to the position of an assistant psychologist and they graduated with grades lower than a 1st class. There were so many other factors which are equally if not more important such as the individual's attitude, values, and work ethic. Academia is not the be all and end all. Graduating with a 1st class is not everything and therefore you should stop killing yourself over it. So, take a moment to pause and think about what your basic needs are, if these are met, and how could these be met. Spend time thinking about how you speak to yourself with respect to your intelligence and the way you study. What is enough and what is acceptable. Really focus on that 'fine line' between what is important for your academic development as well as your personal wellbeing. This will help guide your actions and consequently affect how well you feel and how well you perform.

Graduating with a 2.1 honours degree is perfectly acceptable. It shows a good level of competency and knowledge of the subject which you can build on. Employers and academics would be satisfied seeing such a result as it indicates you have a drive to learn and to develop yourself. Supervisors would also identify that you have areas which you can develop upon and they are able to support this. So, if you are on track for graduating with a 2.1, you are doing well.

I now come to people who are looking at graduating with a 2.2 or below. Such students could realistically face additional challenges as many employers looking to recruit assistant psychologists typically expect a 2.1 as a minimum. However, not all hope is lost. Such students could potentially go on to do additional courses to develop the academic knowledge and thus support their grade. This may mean that individuals might choose to do a further diploma in the subject of psychology or go on to do Master's degree as we will discuss in Chapter 6. It may also be that this group of people would be required to do further voluntary work in healthcare sectors to develop their knowledge and CV. Taking on such actions would support you to becoming better equipped to work as an assistant psychologist. However, graduating with a 2.2 from your undergraduate psychology degree may pose a challenge when it comes to applying for the clinical doctorate training. Again most universities typically look for applicants who have achieved a 2.1; however there are exceptions. For instance, certain universities are willing to accept applicants who graduated with a 2.2 from their undergraduate psychology degree if they have completed a PhD. If you fall into the camp of graduating with a 2.2, it is worth researching the entry criteria for the clinical doctorate training at nearby universities so that you can take the appropriate steps required to be better suited to apply for the training course. Just remember, because you graduated with a 2.2 does not mean that you do not have the capabilities or intelligence of completing a PhD or the clinical doctorate training. It does not mean you're stupid and hope is not lost. There are people who have graduated with a 2.2 and they have gone to do their clinical doctorate training. Therefore, it is absolutely possible, though it may require a bit more thought, time, and effort to build upon academic knowledge and work experience.

There are also a few students who have an interest in pursuing a career in clinical psychology though they did not study psychology for their undergraduate degree. They may have studied another subject like social sciences, philosophy, or humanities. Again, it is absolutely possible for these students to progress and pursue a career in psychology. Generally speaking, this group of people are required to complete a conversion course that is BPS approved, which typically lasts for two years. Although spending time on this conversion course may frustrate some individuals as they wish to progress fast, it is important to hold in mind that pursuing a career in psychology is always possible. Additionally, taking a detour in studies may not be detrimental, and in fact may enhance your scope of knowledge and allow you to think more wholly. I have come across a couple of clinical psychologists who had begun their career later in life, changing from another path, and they were excellent clinicians with rich understanding of human beings.

"When educating the minds of our youth, we must not forget to educate their hearts", Dalai Lama. A final reflection is on the appropriateness of knowing the subject we should be studying and what our career path should look like. For many of us, we have to apply to study at university around the age of 16 or 17 years. That is such a young age and people may not necessarily know what they want to do at that point in their life. Some people have barely gotten out of their mother's womb! It feels ridiculous to expect a 16 year old to know and determine what the rest of their life is going to look like. At the age of 16 years, you are still a child and may not know what to expect or know the reality of pursuing certain career paths. Even your brain has not fully developed to an adult level yet. You as an individual might change, and I would expect people to change during that age. 16 year old you should not be the same as 30 year old you. At 16, you have plenty of time to change, grow, and develop. Your attitudes, perspectives, values, and wants may evolve over your lifespan as you gain more life experiences, meet different people, see new places, and work in different areas. Changing and evolving is perfectly fine and it is healthy. Following what fits best with you, your values, your enjoyment, and your lifestyle is paramount to ensure your wellbeing. This may involve pursuing clinical psychology as a career path or it may involve going in a different direction – and either way is fine, as long as it is true to yourself.

Principle 3:
When there's a will, there's a way. You do not have to be exceptionally academic to be considered to the clinical doctorate training course.

Principle 4:
You change over time and so do your choices. The 16 year old you does not have to determine the future adult you.

CHAPTER 5
What now?

You have graduated from your psychology Bachelor's degree. Congratulations. Celebrating your achievement, you feel you deserve to enjoy the summer break. You might go on holiday, travel, party with friends, or return home to see family. As the summer draws to a close you think, what now? Some of you (in fact, many of you) might have been frantically applying for jobs that feel clinically relevant or applying for further education such as a Master's degree or a PhD. Having a quarter-life crisis, pulling my hair out, not knowing what to do or what life holds, it suddenly dawns on me that I am like any regular Joe out there with a Bachelor degree. Crap. Having a psychology degree didn't make me 'know things at a deeper level' or even 'hip'. It did not mean that I would be able to get a job as a paid assistant psychologist. Hell, I wasn't guaranteed to get a voluntary post as an assistant psychologist. It pretty much felt like a useless piece of paper.

Here I was, stuck and desperate to find a job even if it was in a completely different field, anything, just so I can get paid so I can pay my bills and eat – I wasn't aiming for luxury, just aiming for the bare necessities. After all, beggars can't be choosers. I spent 12-hour days looking at different jobs, clinical and non-clinical, applying for anything I may have been half-qualified to do. At one point, I went down the line of looking into various post-graduate courses including accounting. I managed to progress with the initial stages of accountancy, but then it dawned on me, this is insanely boring. I can't be doing this for the rest of my life. I would rather watch paint dry or even an episode of Coronation Street. It felt like I was expected to have the patience of a saint, suspending my impulse to throw rotting bananas at other people. As if I would ever be so inhibited and controlled. It's like asking me to sit in front of a 12 pack of Krispy Kremes and not eat them, I couldn't do it. But seriously, who knew accountants were so patient and had high tolerance to feelings of irritability in order to do such tedious and remedial work? Gaining such insight, I developed a huge amount of respect for accountants as a whole.

And as you can imagine, any chance I had of developing a career in the world of accountancy quickly ended. Many other people may have had similar experiences in pursuing other career paths and working in said line of work before they find themselves being pulled back into clinical psychology. And that is ok – anything and everything is possible and acceptable.

Back to the grind it was. After submitting a crazy number of applications to jobs that were clinically relevant, I got accepted onto a Master's degree course in clinical psychology. Really? I will be honest, I was surprised I got offered the place given we had to submit an 'original and comprehensive' research proposal within our application form, the project proposal being something I wrote in 20 minutes after being at the pub for a few hours. Wow. I don't even know if what I wrote made sense but I guess at the very least spellchecker rescued me. Well, good thing standards could not have been not too high for admission. My journey continues back in school. As much as I am not a huge academic, at least this was one stage closer to helping me become a clinical psychologist.

I applied for a lot of different clinical jobs and other further education courses before I got accepted onto that Master's degree course. Like me, I presume that a lot of you at this stage would be doing the same – applying for clinical and / or research positions as well as further education. The best thing I could say at this point is keep applying, you will get something in the end. It may be a numbers game, the more you apply, the more likely you will be offered something. It's ok to get a 'no' because the more no's you get means you are getting closer to a yes.

Principle 5:
Don't lose hope. The more no's you get, the closer you are to getting a yes

CHAPTER 6
Higher education: Back to academia

"Competition is everywhere. Just do it, and do it better", M. J. DeMarco.

A Master's degree has become very typical for many people who go on to do the clinical doctorate training. It is not a mandatory requirement, though it seems to have become the 'norm'. This may be reflective of the high competition around getting an assistant psychologist post or getting offered a place on the clinical doctorate training. Attempting to do something in order to 'stand out', a Master's degree feels like a good option, until you begin to realise that you are just 'keeping up with other people'. Ouch. That was definitely the feeling I had when I realised that I was surrounded by highly intelligent people all of whom also wanted to become clinical psychologists. I had a lot of respect for my classmates and they each had excellent and unique qualities. Some of them had even been assistant psychologists. And there I was, nothing unique about me except for my chaotic hair. I was perhaps the person with the least amount of clinical or research experience in that lecture hall. I was not particularly bright and on top of that I probably killed off some brain cells watching cartoons and drawing dinosaurs. How would I ever get a clinically relevant job after this degree if I am just a drop in an ocean?

The grading system just got a whole lot harder

Although I graduated from my Bachelor degree with an overall 2.1 grade, I achieved a 1st class standard in most of my assignments. Instead of facing a 3rd, 2.2, 2.1, and 1st class (lowest to highest grade respectively), there was a new grading system for the Master's degree: pass, merit, and distinction (lowest to highest grade respectively). I thought to myself, given I worked so hard in the past and was able to get good grades, surely, I can do this again. Well, no, not necessarily. After receiving the results of the first assignment I submitted, it felt like someone ripped off my right arm and then beat me with it. I worked so hard on this damn assignment, perhaps the hardest I had to date, and I barely scraped a pass. Great. Either I just got a whole lot stupider or the nature of the education system got a whole lot harder. Apparently, it was the second. One of the lecturers told all students following that assignment hand-in that the expectations were a lot higher and the quality of work would be scrutinised a lot more than what it would have been during the Bachelor's degree. What would have been a 1st class standard was now the equivalent of a pass. Academia got tough. Great. I was starting to get worried they would give us an easy ride. Remembering the melt downs and panic attacks during my Bachelor's degree, I was unsure how I was going to pass this one. I was unsure if I had the competency or skills. I wasn't even sure if I had enough hair on my head to pull out. I was in my infancy.

As the course went on I noticed certain subtleties which supported development. These almost felt like learning experiences and skill development, not necessarily related to the content of the course or modules, but rather the process of completing this type of degree. I was unsure whether or not these learning experiences were intentionally driven by the course because no one ever spoke about it. None of the lecturers expressed that these were skills they wished students to develop and they did not suggest that developing these skills would substantially improve grades. At no point did it feel like lecturers actively 'taught' these experiences, though this was something more innate and integrated within higher education. I was certainly unaware of these lessons during my Master's degree and it is only through observation I have been able to understand these lessons and use them to my advantage. In this section, I am going to share a few primary lessons. These are core principles that can be utilised across any higher education degree, not just specific to the subject of the degree. I share these with you in the hope that they can support your development and perhaps make life that little bit easier. Below I've listed these with a brief description of what the 'lesson' was, why this was helpful, and how this influences your development. These lessons are also true for the clinical doctorate training, so keep them in mind.

- **Lesson 1: Less is more.** Funny isn't it. Typically we believe that the more we read, the more we research, the more we revise, the better we will perform. Surely that should be the way right? Not necessarily. In fact the more we research a particular topic, the more we risk getting caught up in what I like to call 'the web of academic doom'. This essentially involves someone who is keen to learn and perform well (let's face it, if you're reading this book that probably includes you) picking up a piece of research, reading it, then moving onto a second related topic, then a third topic related to the second, then a fourth topic and so on. This creates a sense of information overload which can become incredibly overwhelming and difficult to both understand and retain. People do this in the hope of doing well and showing off how much they know (perhaps in an exam or assignment), but unfortunately they actually do the exact opposite. The information communicated looks messy, it may not make sense, and it can become too convoluted. You're dragging someone else into the doomed web.

  a. Why is this helpful to know? You might want to rephrase the question and ask why would you not want to know this? Would this not save you time and effort? Instead of reading and researching endlessly without purpose and getting tangled up, would it not be best to just step back and look for what it is that is needed? I am not suggesting do not learn or research the topic areas, I'm saying learn only what feels relevant and necessary. Remember the rule used in the NHS about patient confidentiality – as much as this is a different area, the principle still applies – only access what is necessary, never more than what is required. Doing this may help you save hours of stress, keep you from premature balding (or me in this case), and even make the topic clearer in your mind so that you actually understand the subject properly.

  b. How does this influence your development? Knowing you can perform well with less effort may affect how you apply this rule in other areas of life and subsequently, affect the approach you take on in your clinical doctorate training. Putting pressure on yourself to learn as much as possible can become detrimental to your development. If you are able to let go of that pressure and feel safe to do so whilst knowing that there are benefits to identifying and abiding to the limits of 'what you need to learn and know', you can perform substantially better. This can also help you live a life that feels less stressful and chaotic and engage in activities that are meaningful when they need to be.

- **Lesson 2: Focus on depth, not breadth.** This lesson somewhat relates to lesson 1. Learning about a lot of different topics, but perhaps to a lesser degree is worse than learning a lot about a few areas. You may not believe me and academics out there may dispute it, but it's true. It's been proven time and time again across many disciplines inside and outside psychology, aligning with the Laws of the Pareto Principles (if you do not know about this and have spare time on your hands, look it up). I'm not suggesting ignoring entire modules given you will be tested on it at some point, but you only really need to learn about one or two theories inside out along with some references to back it up. Knowing a lot about a fewer number of subjects allows us to understand better, to provide a better argument, and we can be concise and clearer when providing an answer. To the marker, having a lot of different theories and bitty information may look like you are meandering; you're not entirely sure how to answer the question so you've gone for the approach 'let's throw in everything including the kitchen sink'. The beautiful thing about psychology is that, with a little bit of thought and creativity, you can pretty much apply most theories to most problems and case studies. Why not do this really well with one or two transdiagnostic theories, instead of doing it poorly with ten.

a. Why is this helpful to know? You have freedom of choice to ignore my recommendations. No one shackled you to read this or apply it to your academic journey. But if you want to do well without getting spotty skin and losing your temper at your partner, this may be key. And for those of you who have employed this and found it beneficial, you're welcome.

b. How does this influence your development? If you do employ this lesson, you are likely to choose a theoretical approach (or topic area) that fits in with your personality, your views, your values, and your preferences. When you excel at learning about this theory / topic area, you may begin to see it in real life, interactions with friends and family, as well as your work clinically. It gradually makes more and more sense as you come into contact with it more. I don't necessarily want you to be a "psychologist" 24/7, but when you know something, it doesn't fall out of your head. You will simply begin to see similar patterns again and again. This can affect your work with service users, how you are on the doctorate, and even how you develop as a human being and your relationships.

I would have to say I wish I knew these two lessons when I initially started, it would have made my life a lot easier. In addition to the two I mentioned above, there were a couple more lessons which were more obvious but still felt valid to bring up here.

- **Lesson 3: Publish something, they will want it**. If you're into it or not, having your research published is always viewed positively. This lesson is perhaps an obvious one, though it is an important one to remember. It may be arduous and feel taxing particularly when you have got what feels like a mountain of assignments to complete, presentations to prepare, and exams to revise. Completing research and publishing it is possibly one of the last things you want to think about. Pushing it out of your life feels really tempting though doing it can bring multiple benefits. First, your chosen lecturer who is collaborating with you on your study may be well known in the field and who best to have your name next to? Second, having an academic study published in a peer reviewed journal is indicative of the quality of your work, not only when applying to assistant psychologist positions but also the clinical doctorate training. Third, it pushes you to learn a lot on how to conduct high quality research and how to write it in a way that impresses others who are expert in the field. There may be many reasons that are pulling you away from wanting to publish, but think about it: you have to do that damn research project anyway, why not do it well and have it published? Isn't that the point of research to begin with: we study something so we can share it with the world for real life application? You can moan and complain about it all you want, but after you're done with that just get that research paper out to the world.

a. Why is this helpful to know? Bottom line is it helps your professional development. Publishing research in peer reviewed journals can support your application form when getting that first assistant psychologist job or getting on the clinical training. People like seeing it. And your academic tutors will like you for publishing it and may support you further in networking with other professionals in the field.

b. How does it influence your development? Generally speaking it will make you a better researcher and a better author. It will push you to make your arguments clearer when presenting a case (which by the way you will have to do a lot in clinical training as well as when you're qualified). You may even learn you wish to pursue the academic career path, even if it is for a little while. Alternatively, you may learn that this is something you definitely want to stay away from.

- **Lesson 4: You won't always like it, and no one will care**. In reality, there may be several elements to your Master's degree that you won't like or are uninterested in. And no one cares. You have to suck it up and do it anyway. Unfortunately, many of us are forced to do or learn about things that we do not always like or care about. The other side to this is that your academic tutors and lecturers are unlikely to care about your preferences. At this stage you can very easily feel deflated. I certainly don't want you going down the line of learned helplessness as that does not benefit anyone, but I would rather encourage you to think about how could you get by doing something you don't particularly like and being faced with people who don't particularly care about it. There are a few possible options: think of the short timeframe that you will have to learn about this; identify a theory you like which you can apply to this topic; detach emotionally and mentally from this; consider the importance of this area and "what's the point of it". Sadly, there is not a lot more I can say about this except for the fact that it will end. You will eventually get to a point where you actually enjoy what it is you are doing and learning.

a. Why is this helpful to know? I hate to break it to you but this will probably happen a lot throughout your career. You will face various situations, whether that be in higher education, research, or clinical work, where you feel forced to do something that you do not like or care about. As much as this feels rubbish at the time, there is always something to learn from doing this. So, ask yourself: what can I learn from this experience? What would it be like to think "I get to do..." instead of "I have to do..."? This subtle shift in language can open our mind to the opportunity we are given. Thinking about this may make the experience a lot more tolerable, and dare I say, maybe even enjoyable?

b. How does this influence your development? Considering this can help you build your tolerance to engage in work that perhaps you don't necessarily prioritise though it is necessary to your development. You can apply this in subsequent stages of your life and career path to continue developing. Patience is a virtue (if managed and practiced in a healthy way).

Principle 6:

Less is more

Principle 7:

Focus on depth, not breadth

Principle 8:

Publish what you can, your work deserves recognition and to have real life application

Principle 9:

Invest your efforts in that which is most fruitful for you

CHAPTER 7
That b*tch named... People you come across

"The competition is cutthroat, even among best friends. And you have to be able to, by virtue of experience, deal with it", Rush Limbaugh.

Thankfully, the majority of people are nice, helpful, and trustworthy. They embrace the qualities you would hope to see as future therapists and clinicians. But there will always be that one sh*t head you come across. And that person may not always be a student.

But first, let us consider students.

In my academic cohort, luckily most of my peers were friendly people who were willing to help each other and had positive intentions for themselves as well as the peer group. However, one individual who I will not name, was a discrete outlier. This girl had become very pally with pretty much everyone on the course, though she would never come out to social events or spend time with others beyond classes. Maybe she was busy, or it just wasn't her scene? Yeah, maybe. Every effort was made to include her in things that she liked at times that were suitable. She never showed up. As time progressed (and hearing conversations some of us were not meant to hear) it became apparent, she did not actually like anyone on the course. She rarely (if ever) showed her genuine self to others. Much of the friendly conversations she had with other people were very superficial, about make-up or clothes. The times when she contacted any of her classmates was to ask specific questions about assignments, exams, information in lectures etc. To be fair, we all asked help from each other now and again, but it was incessant from her. She seemed to go through the entire year group obtaining all information possible, trying to learn everything that everyone else knew, and never give back. She never responded to messages from other people who asked her for help. Hell by the end of the course she barely responded to anything. She got what she wanted and she was off. I felt used.

The only way I can understand and formulate her experiences and her behaviours is that she was coming from a place where she felt threatened (ooh la la look at me being a 'psychologist'). She perhaps felt that her peers were more intelligent than her, that they knew better, and that she was falling behind. She possibly believed other people were not to be trusted. She may have been in fight or flight mode; aware of the competition getting onto the clinical doctorate training, she did not wish to share what she knew with others, fearing this enhanced their chances while 'automatically' reduced hers. Her primary attachment style may have been avoidant: keep people at an emotional distance in order to be safe, which essentially reflected how she was with her superficial conversations. She developed relationships that were 'functional', fulfilling her need to learn and 'get ahead of the game'.

She was the minority in the cohort, but I'm afraid she was one out of many in history to behave in this way. You may come across such individuals, and if you do, please be careful. Share what you feel comfortable sharing and no more. It's not school and you do not need to give your homework to the class bully so they can copy it. Find your backbone with kindness and stick to it. Also, please do not be like her. Everyone is in the same boat, we are all experiencing the same storm. No one likes a sh*t head.

"Good teachers are costly, but bad teachers cost more", Bob Talbert. And now we come to tutors. Thought tutors would be responsible and respectable adults? You'd hope. Generally speaking yes, they are fine. They are often intelligent, helpful, and may be compassionate. But sadly there is always that one rat who manages to burrow their way through.

I can honestly say that one of the academic tutors was interesting to observe, almost like a case study. I was fascinated by how this individual managed to climb up the academic ladder despite being relatively young. This tutor was clearly intelligent, but unfortunately smug and arrogant about it. Not only this, this individual also believed that somehow the opposite sex would be instantly attracted to them, like a moth to a flame. No thank you. Unfortunately, academia aged this person very quickly, a face full of wrinkles and a belly that had its own gravitational pull. I found this tutor frustrating to be around. I recall one incident where I felt unfairly graded by this individual on an assignment and so I contested it. I had to provide an argument as to why I was contesting and low and behold, when I got marked by another tutor my grade went up. Interesting right? As much as it might be a 'gut feeling' and I have no concrete evidence for this, I felt I was unfairly graded as I did not feed into this tutor's ego. I couldn't. The thought of it was nauseating.

If you come across such a tutor, choose wisely what you do. Be respectful and professional in your communications. And if you do get that 'gut feeling', don't ignore it. More often than not, there is something meaningful behind that feeling. Give yourself permission to challenge something that you do not feel is right. Give yourself permission to voice your concerns as and when they come up, even when this includes challenging people in senior positions. As anxiety provoking and uncomfortable as this may be, you have the right to express yourself, your needs, and what you believe is occurring.

Principle 10:
Don't use people to your advantage

Principle 11:
Be mindful of others in order to preserve yourself from their attack or manipulation

Principle 12:
Give yourself permission to voice your concerns

CHAPTER 8
You vs. yourself

"The reason why we struggle with insecurity is because we compare our behind the scenes with everyone else's highlight reel", Steven Furtick. I wish I knew this a long time ago. Like many other people, I think I was trapped in a perpetual state of comparing myself to everyone else around me. I would question: who was more intelligent, who had more experience, who performed better in assignments or exams, who was more approachable, who had better interpersonal relationship styles, who was more likely to succeed, who was more confident, who was kinder? Though the questions may have changed from situation to situation, the essence remained the same. I always presumed that someone else was (if not most people were) better than me and ultimately, I was worse than other people. I tried to rationalise these thoughts at times and look for evidence for and against such beliefs but frankly the questions and consequential beliefs stayed the same. I could see other people genuinely achieving better grades than me, they were more sociable and had better relationships than I, or they had more experience than me. I could not dispute concrete facts. However, I did compare what I knew about myself, including all my internal emotions and thoughts, with the 'best' of what I saw of other people. Somehow, I screened out all their struggles or possible flaws, either because the other person hid such parts of themselves or I was caught up in confirmation bias.

I remember one particular girl who was in my Master's degree cohort. She was intelligent, popular, approachable, had a picture perfect relationship, and years of being an assistant psychologist under her belt. I, on the other hand, felt I had the same number of brain cells as a piece of tissue paper, struggled with my partner, and had zero clinical experience. Back then, I wished I could have swapped lives with her, not that she would have taken up the trade. I didn't resent the girl, nor did I dislike her. On the contrary I almost idealised her (I know, it's quite weird to say). A couple of years go by and I came to learn how her life perhaps was not as magical as I thought it was. There was a lot of heartache getting those jobs she had, she was insecure about her appearance, and I think her partner had been having an affair. She did not have it as easy as I thought. The point here is that as much as we may compare ourselves to others who we feel are doing better than we are, we do not know what skeletons are hidden in their closet.

"Never discourage anyone who continually makes progress, no matter how slow... even if that someone is yourself", Plato. Do not be making fun or dismissing yourself for your efforts in improving yourself and your life. It is often tempting to fall into a trap of criticising ourselves, particularly when we see other people around us who we believe are more successful than we are. We compare ourselves to others and all this results in us being hurt as we compare our worst self with other people's best selves. This comparison in itself is skewed as we only have partial information rather than the full picture. This in itself leaves us in a problematic situation as we are end up wanting what other people have that we see is so desirable. If we knew the full truth about other people's circumstances and the difficulties they faced, we may begin to empathise with them and understand that they too are human, and like us, they too are simply trying to progress and improve themselves and their life. We may not want the life they have as it may not be as easy as we may have previously thought. You only need to be you. The person who stares back at you in the mirror is the only person to focus on. Even if someone else is doing well, that does not take away anything from you. You are your only point of comparison and if you are doing what is best for yourself in order to better yourself and your life, you will get to a point far beyond what you would have thought was achievable.

Plato's expression extends to how we would treat others. Throughout your journey it is possible for you to encounter situations where you see other people who may be doing 'less well' than you are. They may have failed a particular assignment or exam, or at the very basic they may have asked a question that appeared 'ridiculous' or plain stupid. During my Master's degree, one student had asked another student if they could look over her assignment. The purpose of this was to check it for any spelling and grammatical errors as English was her second language. The other student she had asked to review her paper was incredibly intelligent, there was no doubt about it. Unfortunately, this other student was also quite unkind in that she shared this assignment with other people and had made fun of certain sentences which were grammatically incorrect. Wow. It was horrific to watch. This girl had made the effort to complete a Master's degree in another language! No one should have laughed at her; they should have been proud of her for working so hard to achieve something remarkable. No one should have made fun of her progress, no matter how small they thought it was. Such discouragement only hinders us and the development of humanity. Discouragement of either other people or ourselves opposes the very essence of what being a clinical psychologist or a mental health professional is all about. The earlier you begin to recognise that we can only grow from a place of kindness and encouragement, the better you will feel and the easier your career journey will be.

Principle 13:
Our insecurities come from comparing our worst self to other people's best selves. We may never see other people's struggles. Focus only on yourself.

Principle 14:
Never express negativity of person's progress, no matter how small, including your own progress. Only use the voice of encouragement to further progress.

CHAPTER 9
Applying for an assistant psychologist position

"Hard work without talent is a shame, but talent without hard work is a tragedy", Robert Hall.

Assistant psychologist job applications

How many job applications did you submit before getting your first assistant psychologist post? For me, it was a lot. It was a number probably bigger than 10 but smaller than 1000. Truth be told I don't really remember, but I do remember the feeling that it was a lot. I also remember feeling incredibly frustrated with this. There just seemed to be so many obstacles getting in the way of getting my first job. Here are just a few of the problems I faced when applying for the job:

- The person specification requires you have prior experience as an assistant psychologist.
  - My response: Please explain to me how am I meant to get experience if I need to already have experience? Is it me or is this overlooking a glaringly obvious catch 22 dilemma? I'm trying to hold myself back from using more profanities in this book but seriously...

- The job application window is only open for approximately 13 minutes and 48 seconds.
  - My response: I barely ate breakfast in that space of time. Am I literally meant to be glued to my laptop refreshing the page repeatedly in order to get the 'once in a lifetime' chance of applying? So, I should not have a life? (P.S. unfortunately that last question comes up time and time again, which will be discussed throughout this book). I get it, the jobs are

competitive so they can only be open for a short space of time, but egh it feels like I don't even have the privilege to think...

- The job application will shut after the first 50 applicants
  - My response: After realising the level of competition for one job position, I would promptly have a nervous breakdown. Trying to look at the computer screen with my tear-filled eyes, the pressure intensifies to type my application quicker, smoke coming off the keyboard till a fault with the electrical circuit causes a small fire.

- The rush of writing the application form in order to submit on time / within the 'top 50'.
  - My response: Well, given I barely had time to go to the toilet before the job application window shuts, I thought I better write this one fast. Unfortunately, this came with a sense of fear and worry. Wiping sweat off my forehead and getting ready for an online battle, I pushed forward submitting what can only be described as a lame story of my life filled with desperation for working in this field. Poor grammar fills the pages, spelling mistakes go unnoticed, and it is clear that I did not know what the job entailed. No one likes this desperate moron.

- The job specification feels 'vague'
  - My response: Given I was desperate for relevant experience, I did not particularly care about the field I worked in. However, not knowing the job i.e. where you will be working and what you will be doing, can certainly be a bad start. It negatively impacts your job application and you can be rejected at this stage. However, if by some miracle you get through to interview stage, you might be met with a huge shock. Does not help either you as an applicant or the service.

- I meet most, but not all, the essential criteria.

- My response: At the time I questioned, did it really matter? Can I not apply anyway? This is problematic as it can lead you down various paths: lying on your form, embellishing upon the truth of your work / experience, and being expected to complete tasks far beyond your competency. None of these are good.

- I know the qualified staff member who has advertised the job.
  - My response: Can they do me any favours and pick me? No. It does not work like this (and thankfully it does not for multiple reasons). Do not make it blatantly clear that you know the person who will be reading the application form, otherwise you look desperate and stupid. And like I said before, no one likes that desperate moron.

- The job is far from where I live.
  - My response: "I can make that sacrifice of travelling 5 hours a day. Or maybe I can move (it's ok if I'm far from everyone I know and love)". I don't even need to comment on how ridiculous that sounds. A job is a job, it is not worth sacrificing your entire life. Sitting in a car for 5 hours a day, which is 31% of your day after you remove sleep, is not healthy for anyone.

Any of you have these issues? I am going to presume the answer is yes. It is excruciating, I know. The positions are competitive. It sucks. I remember the first assistant psychologist job interview I went to. At the end of the interview, which by the way was an absolute disaster, the interviewer told me "thank you for coming here today. Just to let you know there were 387 applicants for this job (singular) so well done for getting this far". What? I had to pick my jaw up off the floor. I remember that number distinctly because of how much it shocked me. And the sense I should be 'proud' for "getting this far". Even now I notice this fills me with a visceral response of frustration and agitation. When hearing those words, I was not hopeful I would get the job, but I was even more shocked hearing I should be proud having gotten to interview stage. It was as though I was almost a part of the 'special elite' who were assistant psychologists, I would not quite be at that level. Competition was clearly high, and I could not do any more than what I was already doing.

Getting you to interview stage: Perspective of a qualified clinical psychologist

As a qualified clinical psychologist, I have screened application forms and interviewed people looking to become assistant psychologists. It has been an interesting experience being on the qualified side of the job applications and interviews whilst still remembering what it was like to grovel for an assistant psychologist post. There are certain facts that we cannot get away from and unfortunately, these facts do make the process difficult. However, there are certain things that can be done to put you in a better position.

Competition is high. No doubt this is one of the biggest challenges in this entire process. It is a challenge for both applicants and qualified. The reason it is a challenge for applicants is because you feel like a small fish in a big pond: how can you get noticed? The reason it is a challenge for qualified staff is because so many poor candidates need to be filtered out to identify good candidates, and there is always a risk that the best candidate is ignored as their form came through 'too late' (i.e. after the 'cut off' number of 50 applicants). Here are a few points that would guide you to having a decent application form as well as enhancing your chances of getting an interview.

- Pre-prepare your form
   o Some of you may already do this but I would highly recommend for all of you to do it. This way you are generally speaking ready to apply for the job that you want when it comes up. It can sometimes be difficult to prepare your form before even knowing what the job will be, however there are clear and identifiable themes that appear across all assistant psychologist jobs. This is how to do prepare your application form the best way you can:

1. Look through past jobs that have been advertised and how they describe the person specification requirements. Searching through 5-8 jobs should be sufficient for you to gain an understanding of the ideal characteristics that are sought for this position. List the essential criteria you have identified as necessary skills for the applicant to show.

2. Consider the ways in which you meet the essential criteria for the person specification. SPELL THIS OUT. Make it abundantly clear how you meet each element of the essential criteria. The person who is looking through the application forms has a lot to go through, and if it is unclear or convoluted, the way in which you met the criteria can be missed. Not only that, the person looking at your form may also make a judgement that your communication style is poor and thus consider you inappropriate for the job. Make it clear and they will thank you.

3. Think about how you are going to spell out that you meet the essential criteria. You may choose to do this by (a) stating what the essential criteria is and (b) how you meet it using an example. When writing about your example, you may wish to follow the '3 point' rule: Context, Action, and Result. Context: what were the circumstances in which you were working? Action: what did you do to manage the situation? And Result: What happened? How did you review the outcome? And could you improve on this in future situations. Thinking about these 3 areas may help you tease out your example so that it is comprehensive and well thought out. By doing this, interviewers will also recognise your ability to take action,

reflect upon your work, and evaluate your actions in order improve services and care service users receive.

4. Make notes on your transferrable skills. These are skills that can be used in any setting and for any job. Examples may include good communication, liaising with others, holding compassionate and positive attitudes etc. Given these are generic skills, it can be easy to talk about them in any application form and to prepare your form with these before having seen the job.

5. Mention any distinct features, characteristics, or values you hold which may mean you have a special skill or perspective. For instance, it may be that you are of a different ethnic background and you have lived experience of cultural understanding of mental health. It may be that you have been a carer and thus prioritise service users' voices.

6. After following the above steps, it should become a lot easier and faster to add the specific details of the job you are applying for when it comes up.

- Describe and explain all relevant experience
  o Some of the application forms I have screened have been unclear and easily forgettable. This is because the candidate described their experiences in ways that are either unclear, nonsensical, and irrelevant. Their job application may be written more like a diary that offer perspectives and thoughts on areas of work rather than factual statements relevant to the job description. Like I said earlier, identify the essential characteristics / person specification required and illustrate how you meet these essential criteria with concrete examples. This can help the interviewers have an idea of your experiences and abilities. Do not speak about your thoughts and experiences randomly

without connecting it to the person specification and job description, this is a waste of time and energy. It is seen as irrelevant. And remember, the person on the other side of the form is going through so many other forms; you do not want to make them lose the will to live – they are already on the edge of life screening these application forms. Simply talk about concrete and factual experiences you have that are relevant to the job. This would support your application form and provide you with a better chance of getting an interview.

- Attitudes and values.
  - o Some application forms I have read through have been shocking. I mean really shocking. The attitudes and values expressed throughout have been appalling and quite frankly offensive and derogatory to people who use services. I have seen phrases such as "keep people under control" and "force them to have their medication". Hell no. Are you from the past? If you have this attitude, please put down my book and read no further. This is not the career path for you. And if you don't understand why I am saying this or you are even contesting what I am saying, you seriously need to put my book down. I do not give you permission to read on. I realise I may sound unprofessional but people with such an attitude should absolutely not work in a care based profession. Having such people working in a caring profession would be the pinnacle of unprofessionalism. What is the point of having services if we are going to be stigmatising of our service users? You are not helping the progression of mental health services but rather hindering it. We do not 'force' actions or 'control' people who are users of mental health services; we empower and support.
  - o Be genuine with your attitude and values. What is it that you like about mental health services? Why are such services important to you? What meaning does it have for you? Speak about this from a humanistic perspective. Drop formalities and talk from

the heart. How and why would you want to be a part of services that help or support progress?

- Do not lie.
  - For many people, you might be anxious because you are unclear if you meet the requirements outlined in the job description. Therefore, you are unsure if you should add anything that could be described as "an extension of the truth" in order to ensure you meet the requirements. Let me stop you here. The person on the receiving end of your job application form can tell. They know when you are lying or 'extending the truth'. You may not feel it is obvious but trust me, it is to us. It will not get you far and will only make the person on the other end fed up of your form. Be completely and 100% honest in your form. If you do have uncertainties about certain experiences or skills, it is ok to be honest about this. In fact, this can be viewed as admirable, particularly if you have identified how you could address these areas. In this way, we see that you are self-aware of your skills and acknowledge developmental needs. This is incredibly important as it can allow the interviewers identify how this job would fit in with your skillset, how you can develop further, and where support could be provided. Although it might come from a place of insecurity, saying you know everything there is to know and have done everything there is to do makes you sound arrogant.

- Final notes.
  - Grammar and spelling. It is shocking to see the number of applicants with poor basic English skills. I'm not expecting Shakespeare but how about something that simply makes sense? We even have spellchecker now on most computer software programmes! Please make sure you have used good grammar and you have spelt everything correctly. I know we all have the occasional mishaps, but this really does matter in the application form and you are scored on it. By the way,

misspelling of the word 'psychology' is the biggest embarrassment of all.

o Keep up to date. Ensure your academic and employment history are up to date. This may seem like an obvious one but surprisingly not everyone maintains up to date records.

Principle 15:

"By failing to prepare, you are preparing to fail", Benjamin Franklin.

Principle 16:

The competition is fierce and it can be exhausting. Persevere and embrace the humanistic qualities desired in the field of mental health.

CHAPTER 10
Interview stage for an assistant psychologist position

Now that you have received confirmation inviting you to interview, what do you do? How do you prepare? Some people may go into a state of panic, others go into a state of grandiosity. If you fit into the first category of people, pull yourself up. You are better than what you think. If you fit into the second category of people, get down from that pedestal. Think about yourself and the skills you have which led you to getting the interview. Consider your personal strengths as well as areas that require development. I am going to go through general pointers to prepare for interview as well as doing your best in the interview.

- Research the service as well as best clinical practice and typical ways of working in that particular setting.
  - This may seem like an obvious one, but surprisingly one that is missed by some people who attend interview. Before going into the interview, find out more about the service and the setting. What are the standard ways of working in the setting? How does psychology sit within the service? Are there particular aspects that you need to consider further? For example, when I attended the interview to work in a prison, I considered issues such as prison security, the frequency with which I would liaise with prison officers, and the potential conflicting views and dynamics between officers and healthcare professionals. I researched how risk is managed across disciplines as well as relevant policies within high security settings. Considering and understanding all these areas allowed me to think about what it would really be like to work in this setting and I was able to construct my responses more dynamically throughout the interview.

○ From an interviewer's perspective, it is clear when someone has taken the time to understand what it would be like working in such a setting as well as the areas they wish to consider which will guide their decisions. It is acceptable if the interviewee does not know all the answers to these, however it is imperative that they have awareness of areas they need to consider or learn more about to help them work appropriately and effectively in such a setting.

- Research the person specification: what is required and expected of you
   ○ Again, you would think this is an obvious one but when I have interviewed for positions, some interviewees have shockingly neglected this point. The person specification is clearly outlined in the job application and describes essential and desirable characteristics. Spend time thinking about how you meet these criteria, why this may be relevant to the service, and evidence this with examples of your clinical and academic experience. When prepping for interviews, I tend to think through the following questions in order to structure my response as comprehensively and detailed as possible:
      1. What is the criterion?
      2. Why is this criterion important?
      3. What local or trust-wide policy does this criterion relate to?
      4. What example can I discuss to show I have experience in this?

   ○ Going through an example while reflecting on the above questions, my responses might have looked something like this at the time:
      1. What is the criterion: Experience of working with people who have depression and anxiety.
      2. Why is this criterion important: Prior experience working this population is important because I can understand

some of the challenges these individuals may face, including how they would access services, manage life at home, do activities of daily living, or go to work. I would also be aware of negative feelings they might have about themselves, the world around them, and their future. I would recognise that I may have to liaise with other healthcare professionals to support the individual as best as possible. I would think about the challenges I might face working with the individual including how well may they engage with me, what do I need to do to develop a trusting therapeutic relationship, and how can I help them progress towards their personal goals.

3. What local or trust-wide policy does this criterion relate to: The Community Mental Health Framework for Adults and Older Adults; Safeguarding, Data Protection, and Confidentiality Policies.

4. What example can I discuss to show I have experience in this: Working as a volunteer on a telephone counselling service, I used a non-judgemental approach as I helped the individual express their difficult thoughts and emotions. I used reflective statements and summaries to display empathic understanding of their experiences. I gently used questions to allow to explore other areas of their difficulties, as well as questions of guided-discovery to enable the individual to identify potential solutions to their difficulties. I used a relevant questionnaire (e.g. PHQ-9) before and after the consultation to identify level of distress and review whether the intervention has been helpful. I signposted the individual to other services and materials that may also be helpful for their difficulties.

o Having such a detailed response around why you meet the requirements outlined in the person specification along with examples of how you meet the requirements demonstrates a level of competency. It shows that you have a level of confidence and knowledge in the area. It allows interviewers to identify your style of working as well as how effective your way of working has been. It can also provide the interviewers with an idea of what it would be like to have you as a member of the team and areas in which you would require support for your professional development.

Generally speaking, the interview questions will focus on what has already been mentioned in the job description, identifying how you best meet criteria for this post. On occasion you may be required to complete a presentation or engage in a group activity, of which you would be notified prior to the interview. Use the description in the person specification and job description to guide your preparation and responses to the questions asked. These in essence will be your bible, but you have to do the homework around it. Consider how you are right for the job and display this through your work ethics, attitudes, and considerations. Research areas linked to what is noted in the job description or person specification. If you research policies, aim to understand these, what they mean and how they are employed rather than rote learn what the policy states. If a particular therapeutic approach is used, what features are pertinent to this approach, why is it helpful, and how can you embody this? Interviews are not designed to catch you out but rather to find the best in you. But the interviewers can only do this if you are able to show them the best of you.

As much as there are things that you can do to enhance how you are at interview, there are certain things you should absolutely not do. These are things that would leave interviewers having a bad impression of you and would cost you the opportunity of getting appointed. Some of these may be obvious but again, these are things that I have witnessed as an interviewer.

- Prior the interview, do not approach interviewers informally 'for fun' or to 'get an edge'
  - It is perfectly acceptable to contact an interviewer on the details noted on the job advert to ask them specific details about the job or service if it is not advertised. However, for the love of God please do not approach interviewers with informal nonsensical

babble. This includes sending random email greetings with smiley faces, flowers to the interviewer's office, or a basket of muffins to the team. No this does not give you an edge, you cannot 'bribe' your way into getting the job or being noticed, and I guarantee the interviewers will think less of you before even having met you as you display behaviours that are considered unprofessional.

- Do not lie.
  - o I already mentioned this with respect to your job application, but for the love of God do not lie at interview. It is obvious when you do. It is also obvious if you 'extend the truth'. Interviewers are able to identify when you do this. It is just embarrassing. You do not sound clever or competent. It makes you sound desperate, incompetent, and inappropriate for the job.
  - o If you do not know the answer, be honest in that you do not know the answer. Talk about the process you would undertake to find out the answer as well as what you might be hypothesising and how you would test this out. No one knows the answer for everything and that is ok. Qualified clinical psychologists are aware that you are in the early stages of your development and would expect you to not know everything. If anything, they may be stunned if you told them you understood everything. This may raise the question of "well if you know everything, why haven't you been accepted onto the course?". This may lead to doubts about your abilities as well as questions around your honesty, attitude, and self-awareness. Qualified clinical psychologists want you to be willing to learn, to have an open mind, and to be aware of your areas of incompetency. Showing that you are able to take the steps to problem solve challenging situations that require skills and knowledge beyond your competency is crucial.

- Do not use slang or inappropriate phrases.

- ○ Examples of this include "you get me", "like" at every other word, or even "lad" –excuse me, I am a woman. Reasons why this language is inappropriate should be apparent. It does not leave a good impression, the point you are trying to make becomes more and more vague, and it leads interviewers to think your communication style is poor.

- Do not ask inappropriate questions
  - ○ At the end of the interview, the interviewers will give you an opportunity to ask them a question. Usually these questions feel appropriate and are relevant to the job, for example, what does supervision look like, how many clients would I be working with, what are the challenges working here. However, there are some candidates who ask some unusual and inappropriate questions – a few of these include "how old are you?" or "how long have you been qualified?". I fail to see how this is relevant and it only reflects what is going on in your mind: perhaps a reflection of you negatively judging your future supervisor on their age, resentment of your stage in development, or your sense of entitlement for the job. FYI, this is a bad quality to have and will not get you far. It is important that you use this opportunity at the end of the interview to show your interest and your eagerness to help and improve the service in whichever way you can. Asking things like "can I get the bus here?" may be relevant for you, but this will only result in the interviewer going one of two ways: they will either quickly forget you or remember you for putting the job low down on your priorities list.

Principle 17:
Prepare, prepare, and prepare again

Principle 18:
Be sincere with your competencies and humbly recognise personal areas that require development

CHAPTER 11

So, you are a big shot assistant psychologist?

"I got the job"

Congratulations! You're on your first step to becoming a clinical psychologist. Your first day at work resembles something like your first day at school. Nervous and unsure as where to go, what to do, and what to wear, you decide to turn up very early and discover you have to go to a week-long induction. Sitting in boring talks from people who seem proud to have stayed in their job for 20+ years, you cover your mouth or pull a weird facial expression to hide the fact you are yawning all the way through. Isn't it bad enough you didn't sleep well last night, but Mr Toupee at the front of the room is also putting you to sleep? Getting over this hurdle, you then must begin your online competency courses and tests, only to find that you are finding these confusing and hideously dull that you decide to skip straight to the test and Google the answers along the way. Brilliant, looks like you scored 100% without learning anything. The wonders of technology.

You finally discover your office space, where you will be based as an assistant psychologist. For many services, particularly in the NHS, you will most likely have to hot-desk and be ready to get up and leave if someone 'more important' needs to use the office space. That doesn't matter because now you finally got the job as an assistant psychologist! You meet your supervisor and the team and in the hope of making a good impression, you attempt to show off your skills and talk about how keen you are to get involved and perhaps change the world. Ah what a young, innocent, and naïve soul. So full of hope and excitement. It's a shame that will soon end.

Lazy vs. neurotic

"The world is full of willing people; some willing to work, the rest willing to let them", Robert Frost.

Like me, many of you will feel privileged that you got your first job as an assistant psychologist. You recall all the tiresome efforts you spent applying for jobs and attending interviews, feeling grateful that you have finally been given an opportunity to work in this field and get your foot in the door to develop your career. Interestingly, I have also come across other people who appear to be self-entitled, righteous, and almost ungrateful that they have this position. These two sides reflect 2 ends of a spectrum around contentiousness and diligence around their work. One end of the spectrum encompasses people who appear neurotic to some extent, working every moment of every day, while the other end captures people who could not be lazier if they tried.

Personally, I was on the neurotic end of the spectrum. "I lived at work and visited the house sometimes", author Unknown. For me, self-sacrifice became the rule, not the exception. This statement describes my entire journey as an assistant psychologist. Prior to my first job, I was so desperate that I was more or less euphoric when I was appointed following the interview. I didn't care what job I got, just enthusiastic that I got a job. I came from a mental place of scarcity, where I felt that such positions were few and far between, that I had one shot and I would turn into nothing if I was unsuccessful. A weird fight for survival sensation came over me and I believed I had to sacrifice all elements of myself if this meant I could be successful in this line of work. Unfortunately, there are realities to some of what I am saying: there are times when the jobs are few and far between and there are times when it does feel as though you have to self-sacrifice. As you can imagine this has a detrimental effect on your wellbeing as the work-life balance gets thrown out of the window.

The first assistant psychologist job I was offered was part-time working 3 days a week. You would think I would have free time (i.e. 2 days a week) to either develop other skills, look for another job, or to 'relax' if I really had nothing else going on for me. Unfortunately, this was not the case. Even though I had been employed 3 days a week due to limited funding, I was so desperate to impress supervisors and make the project I was working on a success that I worked above and beyond these hours. I used to go in early, some days I would even turn up to work around 7.30am and leave at 7.00pm. I sometimes went in on my days off to finish off other pieces of work and meet service users. I skipped meals, didn't have time to see friends or self-care like go to the gym, and I was sleep deprived. All of this to ensure that I was doing my absolute best at work to 'prove' myself. Self-sacrifice was definitely my 'state of normality' whilst my own needs were discarded. I persevered even when I felt physically unwell to the point that one day I ended up vomiting on myself at work and I was unable to drive home. Searching for someone to help me as most people had gone home by this point, I found one person who happened to be a senior professor left in the building. Well that was awkward and I'm pretty sure I didn't leave a good impression on him. As much as I don't embarrass easily, a part of me hopes he does not remember this incident or even me – the girl who had vomit all over herself because she can't work out when she's too ill to work. Clever.

I need to be clear, none of my incessant working was instructed by my supervisors, this was all me. Some of my friends have referred to me as a "workaholic". I recognised I worked hard, but it did not come from a place of wanting to work or enjoying work to such an extent. It came from a place of feeling it was imperative I do whatever it takes to succeed in this line of work and to demonstrate how hard I worked and that I deserved to be there. It absolutely came from a place of feeling threatened, my fight or flight response was in full swing and I was willing and perhaps even keen to self-sacrifice in order to succeed in a world of scarcity. I got to my breaking point one day and I remember it so vividly. I had just visited a service user at a clinic in the community and I drove back to my base at the hospital site. As I parked my car, I received a phone call from a healthcare professional, shouting down the phone that I was consuming so much of his time by sending letters to him. The letters I had sent related to safeguarding concerns I had around a particular service user under his care and I was so anxious I wanted to ensure everyone involved in the patient's care were aware of these concerns. I explained myself and apologised for consuming so much of his time as he was already aware of these safeguarding issues. After hanging up the phone, I sat in my car and I cried because I was so miserable, not only in my job but overall life. I felt that despite how hard I tried and how much I felt I was doing the right thing, it always felt wrong in the end. For example, turning up to work early and leaving late was 'wrong' as my supervisors were nervous I would ask for extra pay (which by the way, I did not). Informing other professionals about safeguarding issues felt 'wrong' because they were already aware of these concerns. It felt as though there were never enough hours in the day to correct what I had 'wronged' and no matter what I did, I was constantly playing catch up trying to resolve the issue or make things better.

The most significant wrong-doing I did was to myself. I was punishing myself and in the process of self-sacrificing, I also neglected my own basic needs almost as though I did not deserve these. I barely looked after myself, ate poorly, slept poorly, my physical health suffered, and my social life pretty much died. I was destroying myself and for what? No one at work particularly recognised that I was working as hard as I could or that it made a difference. Plus, because I was working myself so hard into the ground I became useless at work – you can't do anything if you are not well yourself. This is completely ironic. The very nature of mental health services is to support people and allow people to develop the ability to care for themselves. However, as employees, we unfortunately neglect ourselves in the process of supporting and caring for other people. I don't regret my actions during this phase of my life because it taught me something extremely important that I will carry forward for the rest of my life: if I do not care for myself, no one else will care for or about me. That is an extremely sad reality but still a reality. And strangely, this is a theme that runs across all stages of your career to becoming a clinical psychologist, and even beyond qualifying.

The lesson here for those of you who are more contentious and work extremely hard, please make sure you are looking after your own self and be sure to do this from the start of your career. If you are not ok, both your physical and psychological wellbeing will deteriorate, and from there it is just a downward spiral. You will struggle to do things that were once manageable to do or even relatively easy. Your work will begin to suffer, and more crucially, your own personhood will be negatively impacted. The hours in the day are limited and your energy is finite; there is only so much work you can possibly do within the hours you are given and aiming to do more is not possible nor is it sustainable. Your energy will deplete and you will just become resentful of your work. More disturbingly, you may begin to resent yourself for being so hard on yourself or for neglecting your basic needs. What is the point of doing work and developing a career if you as a human being are not ok? You are your own foundation and if you do not feel stable, then nothing else built upon the foundation will matter as it will all come crashing down. Be aware of your own wellbeing, check in with yourself often, and do the things you need to do to keep well. There is a definitive line between healthy wellbeing and work which needs to be respected so that we do not fall into the dark abyss.

There is a fine but very obvious line between working excessively and not doing your job. Unfortunately, you can come across colleagues (and chances are these are other assistant psychologists) who are just plain lazy. They do not do very much whilst at work and attempt to avoid the 'hard stuff'. This might include difficult conversations with service users or with other staff members, clinical assessments and reports that need to be completed, or data analysis within research. They may get to a position whereby they feel comfortable at work, they clock in and out, take many breaks in between, and review updates on their social media accounts. They may be 'willing' to allow other people to take on their work who do it for the good of the service, and so they can sit back and relax. Would you like me to get you a mojito while you're sat there? How about I peel your grapes? Luckily, these people are the minority rather than the majority of assistant psychologists, simply because there is a sea of people who are fighting for that job and so interviewers tend to have a 'good sample' to choose from. Frustratingly, these people do exist. They can talk the talk at interview stage which gets them the job, but as soon as they get their contract through they can let their hair down and attend to more important matters like their fashion display show at work the next day. It is safe to say that these people tend to be the ones who take a longer time to successfully get accepted onto the clinical doctorate training course. This is because their lack of work translates to lack of experience which is evident when institutions review applications and at the interview itself. There are a multitude of reasons why you should stop such avoidance of your work and just do it and do it to your best ability. These include: you will develop more knowledge and skill engaging in relevant tasks, you will become more competent and confident in your abilities, you will recognise areas of weakness and ways in which to improve these, you will develop professionally and personally, you will gain more respect from your colleagues, the service users will gain a better experience and improvements will become apparent, you will be supporting service development, and you will support the psychology team to gain validation from the rest of the multidisciplinary team. Maintaining your avoidance of work for a comfortable existence will just be detrimental to yourself and make other people dislike you. Don't be that person. Remember, "the most important actions are never comfortable", Tim Ferris.

'Admin' vs. 'over-competent'

Anyone else get this? This is the weird divide you will find across teams, but hopefully not across clinical psychologists.

With the vagueness of the job role of an assistant psychologist, what they can and can't do, clinical teams end up being baffled and sometimes torn. Some teams end up treating assistant psychologists as administrative staff while other teams treat assistant psychologists as qualified psychologists. Either extremity of this spectrum is not good. It is inappropriate, devalues or overvalues the ability of the individual, and can stunt their professional development. In some teams, I have witnessed assistant psychologists being used purely as administration staff; asked to type up, print documents, scan documents, laminate documents, organise offices, and even tidy up staff rooms. In such circumstances it has been rare that assistant psychologists have been employed to utilise their clinical skills or have been supported to develop clinical skills. Unfortunately, this is such a waste. There are people who use clinical services and we as professionals need to serve service users as best as we can. This includes utilising our clinical skills and maximising staff involvement to enhance the wellbeing of service users. I know, I know, we all need to print out a document on one occasion or another, but that should not be central to our job role. Not only does this let down the assistant psychologist but it also lets down service users.

On the flip side of this, I have seen other teams who treat assistant psychologists as though they are qualified, asking them for their professional and clinical opinion of how to work with service users and manage safeguarding issues. Under the appropriate guidance and supervision of a qualified clinical psychologist, assistant psychologists are able to support the staff team to think about service users in ways that are more psychologically informed. But that phrase is key, "under the appropriate guidance and supervision of a qualified clinical psychologist". Assistant psychologists may be forward thinking, psychologically minded, and have the service user's best interest at heart; however, they are still infants in the stage of their career. They have not yet developed the skills or competency to think comprehensively about clinical, therapeutic, or safeguarding issues. There is a reason why the process to become qualified takes such a long time. You need time and experience to develop such skills. Asking an assistant psychologist to manage and / or give guidance on clinically complex situations is poor recognition of their capabilities and stage of their development. Colleagues within the multidisciplinary team who are confused about the level of competency of an assistant psychologist may believe that the assistant is capable of a lot more than what is appropriate, thus asking them to engage in higher-level work. An assistant psychologist accepting such a request is a dangerous individual with little self-awareness of the limits to their competency and who may be perhaps scared to say so because they don't want to be seen as stupid.

Be aware of your own competency, your strengths and weaknesses, as well as the skills you wish to develop. You know those yearly conversations you have with your supervisors around what key competencies you have and what you want to develop over the following year? Most people sadly treat this as a tick box exercise. Please don't do that, use this opportunity to actually identify what is useful to your development and what would inhibit your development. You are there for a reason. Qualified clinical psychologists are well aware of your stage of development and, presuming you do want to become qualified, want to help you to develop skills that would make you a good candidate for the clinical training doctorate. Find humble strength and wisdom to say no to activities that stunt your growth and that are outside your work remit, but also ask for work projects and guidance around areas that are appropriate for you and that will help your professional development.

"No one is an overachiever. How can you rise above your level of competency? Everyone is an underachiever to different degrees. The harder you work, the more luck you will have", John Wooden.

Being belittled is another rule, not the exception

"You don't have to disrespect and insult others simply to hold your own ground. If you do, that shows how shaky your own position is", Red Haircrow.

This one is another interesting and painful point that some of you may experience being an assistant psychologist. Unfortunately, staff from various disciplines and staff higher up in the chain of command do belittle assistant psychologists which can be a very demeaning experience. It is unclear why this might be; whether it is because other staff do not understand your job role, they do not understand the level of knowledge and experience you have, or they do not know what you can and cannot do in accordance to your level. I have witnessed other staff members from the nursing discipline where they are disapproving of assistant psychologists as they may see them not engaging in certain tasks that they would expect or hope them to, without understanding that this is not within their remit of work. I have also witnessed unit managers who may belittle and become derogatory towards assistant psychologists though this may be a projection of their personal struggles, reflecting their own frustrations and perhaps a level of arrogance. I am also unsure whether the title 'assistant' suggests that the individual is any 'less' or inadequate; however, this should not be the case as assistant psychologists are a great asset to any team and it is unfortunate if such misperceptions occur.

When I was an assistant psychologist, there were times other members of the team including nurses, medics, and social workers were dismissive of me and my work. It felt as though my work was viewed to be of little value because it was done by 'an assistant'. This too goes hand in hand with the concept of self-sacrifice. The more we perceive that our work is inadequate, the harder we will work in order to be good enough. However, if the perception of inadequacy is enforced by other people as others appear dismissive over your work, we are going to work even harder to the point of self-deprecation. And before you 'jump to a solution', no Cognitive Behavioural Therapy (CBT) techniques are of use here. Sitting there looking at 'evidence for and against' other people being dismissive of you and belittling your work will only result you in compiling evidence that people do in fact dismiss you and do belittle you. Often that feeling we get from other people is indicative of something – either something that person is projecting and / or a vulnerability in you that the person is projecting into. Remember that time I talked about the healthcare professional who called me shouting that I was wasting his time? Unfortunately that type of interaction can happen and for some professionals, they express themselves frequently in this way. Unprofessional, yes. As a human being receiving this message, excruciating. Hopefully and thankfully, this is not the case everywhere as many services highly value the work of assistant psychologists and recognise the job role as an important part of the team. I hope that this is the experience that most people have. For people who faced more difficult and challenging colleagues, I sincerely hope such team dynamics improve. News flash: regardless of who you are and your title, we are all humans and should be treated with dignity and respect – all the way up and down the employment hierarchy. If staff members are unable to respect fellow colleagues, then I do not even want to imagine how they are towards service users.

The story of a monk returning the gift of anger. A monk was once giving a speech and a man among the crowd was shouting with anger at the monk. The monk ignored the man and continued with his speech. When asked why he did not respond to the angry man, the monk responded, "if you give a gift to someone and they do not accept it, who does this gift belong to? The gift would return to the person who planned to give it to someone. The same principle works here: if someone is giving you their anger and you do not accept it; it returns back to them".

Perhaps depressingly, this does not necessarily stop when you become a trainee clinical psychologist or qualified clinical psychologist. Sorry to break the news to you guys. The pile of sh*t attitude towards you keeps on smacking you in the face from various directions. Since qualifying, I have had staff members across disciplines and job titles belittle my professional decisions and clinical work, as well as actively going against me and my work with service users. And for what? It is sad really because this is essentially a reflection of them and their unhappiness. That is right, as a qualified clinical psychologist I sometimes formulate specific staff members or clinical teams to understand what is happening. This at least allows me to find empathy towards them which in itself reduces my frustration with them, as well as guide me to navigate such toxic environments. If the venomous words and actions continue, I guess they must have forgotten about the work that I have done to get here. In this case I can just gently remind them that it is Dr Davies to them, not Sarah. They don't like it? We can play the power dynamics game all day long. Of course, I am joking, I would never do this though it can feel easy to get sucked into a power play (which by the way I must say that many male clinical psychologists automatically get addressed by their Dr title, I wonder why... more on this later). It is never worth getting embroiled in the battle of power. It doesn't really help anyone in the end and gives them permission to fuel their argument.

In one of the hospitals I worked in a qualified clinical psychologist, a nursing assistant really did not warm to me. She was incredibly cold and distant; she never attended any discussion groups I held with the staff team and she never actioned any plans I made with the team to support service users. She would not even say hello to me or even recognise my existence, though she was ultra-friendly and chatty with the rest of the nursing team. What a cow. After working with her for a few months, I discovered her terribly dark secret... Want to know what it is? She wanted to be a psychologist at one point in her life. I believe she tried a few times but did not succeed. When looking at her with a formulaic lens, it was obvious why she was so bitter towards me. I was around 15 years younger than her, qualified, and arguably better looking (hah, I am going to take this compliment while my wrinkles are at bay!). Feeling rejected from the field of psychology, this would have created a lot of emotional distress for her, making her question if she was good enough, intelligent enough, or likeable enough to ever be accepted in this line of work. This would not only have made her doubt her occupational skills but it would have also made her doubt herself as an individual, her values and her persona. As much as she may never have wanted to talk to me about it, I can imagine this would have really hurt. Despite how she treated me, I could see that she could be a nice person and had good qualities. She was friendly (not to me of course, but she had that ability to be), she was thoughtful, and she could problem-solve difficult situations. However, she did have one characteristic flaw, and this was a big one. She could not tolerate any level of criticism. Her defences were activated and would have her rifle ready to fire at anyone who criticised her. She would argue till the bitter end, even if the argument no longer made rational sense. I know criticism can be hard to hear but the sad part was that she would become defensive even when it was not necessarily critical but rather a request for her to do something differently. She perceived such situations as personal criticisms. On a number of occasions, when developing care plans with service users alongside the team, she was the person who ultimately ignored these actions and did whatever she thought was best. In her mind, she knew better. Regardless of how gentle I was with her to not destroy her ego, I barely got anywhere. But I guess with an attitude like that, it is no wonder that she did not succeed as a psychologist.

It takes two people to engage in a difficult interaction. Notice what you can control and accept what you cannot control. Notice what you can continue working on that is important for you, your job role, and ultimately for the people who use our services. Notice the level of insight and the experiences people who belittle, attack, and reject us have. Doing these can help you manage such difficult situations and give yourself permission to say 'no thank you' to their negativity.

Principle 19
Developing skill and competency does not come easy. It takes determination and hard work.

Principle 20

Be aware of your own competency and work to your limits, seeking help and guidance where you need it.

Principle 21

People often project onto others what is actually a reflection of their internal state. Hold this in mind, return any negativity projected, and hold onto your own personal strength

CHAPTER 12
Surviving other assistant psychologists

'The assistant club'

"Mature people do not threaten to hurt people, start rumours, seek attention, start pointless drama, gossip behind backs, and overreact to every little thing. That's immaturity", author Unknown.

The joys of observing a clique of assistant psychologists. I was never someone who particularly liked attaching myself to a 'group' of people anyway, like the popular crew in school, but somehow groups of assistant psychologists appeared a lot worse. You would think that popularity contests and b*tching would have ended at high school but no, adults do this too. If anything adults have had years of experience to perfect this skill. Even adults who work in healthcare settings. Sigh. I just think their lives must be so empty. As an outsider looking in, to succeed within such cliques would require as much effort as working a second job. It looked exhausting and I know it would drive me insane. No thanks.

From what I have witnessed, many of the cliques appeared to have three main features: popularity, destruction of others, and competitiveness. Just like high school, n'est pas?

- **The popularity contest**. Generally speaking, most people who enter healthcare professions wish to do this because of an internal desire they have to care for others, to show compassion and kindness towards humanity. People also may approach this line of work to fulfil their own personal needs and desires including learning more about and caring for themselves. However, weirdly this appeared to generate some sense of 'popularity' with respect to 'who is seen to be the most likeable, the most approachable, or the kindest'. Some assistant psychologists worked really hard to be liked by other people, colleagues and service users, by presenting themselves as 'ultra-kind', 'ultra-generous', and 'going the extra mile'. It's true, we can all be kind, generous, and go the extra mile to help our colleagues and service users and I would advocate people doing this in order to nurture each other and grow in a direction that is most meaningful. However, with people who were trying to win the popularity contest, the undercurrent of falseness within their actions was pungent. These individuals would interestingly be very selective as to whom they displayed this level of kindness, generosity, and effort. They would tend to select people who they believed were 'influential'. At times, it was almost like watching a groupie, seeing who is the biggest fan of the consultant or professor so they could have that oh so special moment of spending time with them. Intimate. Will that help you climb up the professional ladder? Maybe, but if it does then I would say shame on the consultant or professor. This reminds me of one professor who became romantically involved with an assistant psychologist as she drilled her way through to his heart. She was desperate to win the popularity contest; she was so persistent, insistent, and obsessive. This girl had the same style as a woodpecker. I think other people in the clique just had to let her win: it would have been a losing battle to challenge her. She was fighting to be popular among her colleagues through attempting to be the most beautiful, the skinniest, the most intelligent (and possibly the most annoying, which in my mind she won by a landslide). As much as other people within this group were attempting to win the popularity contest, this girl took it to a whole new level. She wore boob tubes (remember those?!) with short shorts and short skirts to work on most days to show off her 'hot body' and attract older male professionals. Surely it must have been a nightmare inside her head to be constantly working at being popular. Unfortunately, this turned on her as she quickly and secretively became unpopular in the group. People did not wish to confront her about how ridiculous she was being, because let's face it British people like to be conservative and avoid the reality of the subject. What she was doing ended up going against her. Don't be like her: it's not good for your sanity, it may create problematic interpersonal dynamics with others, and you simply lose your integrity along the way.

- **Destroying other people.** Do you know the story of Queen Cleopatra? She had her siblings killed in order to become the ruler of Egypt, and she succeeded. A similar theme runs through some of the assistant psychologists, in that they feel it is necessary to destroy other people in order for them to succeed. What a beautiful goal to have. One way of establishing a successful-unsuccessful or popular-unpopular dynamic is through destroying other people and their esteem. Sad, right? Unfortunately, this happens even within healthcare roles, the epitome of irony in this setting. This can occur in various ways. The person may: be critical about you behind your back, they may make direct snide comments, they may choose to 'get in the way', or they may simply not help when you are struggling. It is like being 13 years old again on the school playground. Remember that girl I mentioned earlier who got into the relationship with her professor? Her behaviours were a classic example of this. What is funny is that although I was a qualified clinical psychologist and she was an assistant, I noticed she would occasionally attempt to assert herself towards me by attempting to knock me down a few pegs. B*tch please, who do you think you are? The scary part is that she is not the only person like this out there who is trying to become a clinical psychologist. It shocks me to think that there are people with this characteristic who are attempting to become senior members of staff in healthcare settings. Having a destructive attitude towards others is the anti-care. I sincerely hope that through evolution, these individuals get filtered out of the ecosystem. And with respect to this girl, the last I heard was that she still has not got on the clinical doctorate training and is pursuing other options. Well that is fortunate.

- **General competitiveness.** This is perhaps the epitome of all characteristics assistant psychologists possess. In order to succeed in a fiercely competitive profession, you are going to have to be competitive yourself. Everyone hops into survival of the fittest mode, working at their highest level and perhaps destroying others they see around them. Yes, that even occurs in the 'assistants club'. You get lulled into a false sense of security and bam, when the time comes, they strike with sneaky ways of beating you down so they can run ahead. It upsets me that I even had to write about this section in all honesty, but this is the sad truth. Because getting into the profession is so competitive, people end up behaving in ways that are alarming and that may be against how they view themselves and their personal values. They may generally be kind and thoughtful people in their own personal lives and communities however when it comes to applying for jobs or the clinical doctorate training, all niceties are forgotten and primal instincts kick in. This desire to survive and succeed is tied in with another characteristic that the majority (if not all) of the people who succeed in this line of work possess; high standards. Most psychologists I have met have exceedingly high standards of themselves and they work towards perfectionistic levels. As much as we support service users to let go of perfectionism because no one is perfect and striving for perfectionism can lead to the sense of consistent failure, we are the ones who possess a drive for perfectionism the most. Classic example of do as I say, not as I do. There is a very real dilemma within this process: the field is competitive so in order to succeed you would have to have perfectionistic standards in order to be the fittest of them all. However, by having perfectionistic standards, you can never be good enough. And if you are not good enough, your perfectionistic standards bump up even more given the competition you see around you, causing you to work harder and harder but always feeling like a failure. A vicious cycle created by the very profession of clinical psychology. Is this the secret? That actually clinical psychology creates problems that people never had and then create solutions to these problems, essentially to keep us in business? Interesting thought eh? Maybe I should write another book about that one...

You can see that these features can be incredibly toxic and exhausting, but unfortunately these are characteristics possessed by many assistant psychologists. Although many 'lone' working psychologists can display these characteristics, they are significantly compounded within the 'assistants club'. The 'club' may essentially start off as a forum for support and individuals within the group have good intentions wishing to help others and in turn receive support. However, it can very quickly and very easily turn sour because of the characteristics outlined. So please be careful. Engage with others on a level that feels healthy, safe, and appropriate, but be mindful of times when it becomes overwhelming and toxic. The profession is hard enough as it is, no one needs to become sucked into that way of being.

The assistant psychologist group

Oh the groups. These groups may not be all over the country, but in some locations assistant psychologist groups are organised by assistant psychologists and / or clinical psychologists for assistant psychologists to attend and meet one another. The purpose of these groups is generally to support one another around career development and applying onto the clinical doctorate training course. On the surface, these groups may seem like a really good idea. It might appear that these groups are really helpful in that people who attend would share advice and would have your best interest at heart. Did that sound suspicious when I said that? That other people (including other assistant psychologists) would have your best interest at heart? Well, if it did sound suspicious that's because chances are there is something a little more sinister going on behind the curtains, similar to what I reflected upon earlier – you will unfortunately come across people who are willing to trample on you in order to increase their chances of success. However, these groups are not all negative. It is genuinely mixed as to how useful you would find these groups with respect to your knowledge, career development, and application form, as well as your own mental wellbeing and how you view yourself and others. Obviously, it's entirely up to you whether or not you decide to attend these groups. Reflecting on my own personal experience as well as other colleagues who have been assistant psychologists, I've indicated some pros and cons around these groups. This might not be an exhaustive list and it might not reflect everyone's experiences who attends these groups; however, these may help you navigate the assistant psychology groups and consider where you would prefer to focus your time and energy.

Pros:

○ *Useful information.* The benefits of attending these groups is that you can occasionally get some useful information about various areas that would be relevant to your career development. Such information may include:

1. *How to approach the application form for the clinical doctorate training.* There are occasions whereby discussions are held among the group and a presentation by assistant psychologists, trainee clinical psychologists, or qualified clinical psychologists follows. Within these discussions and presentations, they may discuss the characteristics of which you need to embody when approaching the form. This may include important values and attitudes that you would have as a mental health professional. Examples include showing compassion and care to other individuals, prioritising person-centred care, and ensuring safety along with evidence-based practice. Discussions may also include how you view services and how to express these views in your application form to indicate that you wish to enhance and support best practice. They may also discuss the fine line you are treading by displaying a good level of competency though remaining humble to recognise your limits and areas of incompetency. These are all really important areas to consider particularly when completing your application form for the clinical doctorate training (or any other job application for that matter). As much as it is useful to consider these areas, at times these discussions may lack

detail and depth. Therefore, it is important that you take time out after such discussions to reflect upon such areas, either with other people or independently, so that you develop more confidence in this area.

2. ***Key words and phrases to note and reflect upon in the application form.*** Many individuals completing the application form for the clinical doctorate training believe that there must be some sort of secrete combination of words and terms that provide an indication to reviewers that they are a good candidate and should be interviewed. Well, if there is a code, I haven't been able to crack it and neither have a lot of other qualified psychologists or lecturers on the training programme. There isn't a code. We all know that there are certain key words and phrases that are important to consider and include to display best practice, competency, and one's values. These may include implementing evidence-based practice, developing a therapeutic relationship, collaborative working, liaising with the multidisciplinary team, safeguarding, utilising supervision etc. Attending these groups may help you think more about these terms, whether you have practiced these in your work, and how you would describe such practice in your form.

3. ***Therapeutic approaches and research projects.*** There are times when the group discusses particular therapeutic approaches and / or research projects that are currently undertaken by certain organisations or trusts. These tend to be helpful to sit in as this provides you with an opportunity to develop your general knowledge about ongoing practice as well as new developments. This can also inspire you to develop your career in particular directions that resonate more with your personality type and preferences.

4. ***Assistant psychologist jobs.*** Individuals within these groups may also speak about new assistant psychologist jobs that will be advertised. This may be because someone has left their assistant psychologist post, new funding has been approved for an additional post, or a new service has been established. Discussing such opportunities with individuals may help you think more about your job application form if you are wanting to apply for another assistant psychologist position. Knowing more about new upcoming opportunities can help you consider your skill-set, knowledge, and competency, and how you could be an appropriate candidate for the such jobs.

o ***Support from others & friendships.*** I personally did not experience this, but I can imagine there is a possibility that some people attending this group would get on well with one another and develop a friendship and / or be able to provide support to one another throughout their career journey. Even though I did not personally come across this, and other people among my cohort did not report having such experiences, I believe that anything is possible – and attending these groups lends itself to this possibility more than if you never attended.

Cons:

o ***The people you meet aren't all that.*** It takes all kinds of people to make the world. As much as many people who are assistant psychologists are thoughtful and contentious, unfortunately that does not apply to all people you come across. Remember I spoke about those people who are trying to win the popularity contest? Those people in constant competition? Or those people who lost their conscious and are willing to trip up others? All those people come to the assistant psychologist groups as well. This place is an opportunity for such individuals to have their ego stroked by their peers (or themselves). They voice their knowledge and take the stage to express their superiority to others. It's hard to feel comfortable when surrounded by such people.

○ ***Breeding ground for anxiety, doubt, and low mood.*** Generally speaking, most "normal" people attend this group in the hope that information they learn would 'give them an edge', increasing their chances of being a successful applicant to the clinical doctorate training. All individuals sit there eagerly listening and making notes, craving the magic formula to success. As they meet other people, they become aware of the competition they face and suddenly it becomes a fight for survival and only the fittest of the fit would win glory. As people differ and are unique in their qualities, attitudes, behaviours, and interactions, chances are you will come across people who are highly competitive and cut-throat. As those individuals express their superiority and come across as intimidating, you begin to feel smaller and smaller while your level of incompetency somehow magnifies. Being in such a situation can lead you to believe that you are simply 'not good enough', that there are other people who are better than you and are perhaps more worthy. You may feel that other people are more knowledgeable, experienced, eloquent, and a 'better fit'. This sense of 'not being enough' can lead you to all kinds of dark alleyways in your mind and could affect how you see yourself as a human being, that perhaps you will never succeed and that the situation is hopeless. In this sense, you become riddled with anxiety, doubt, and low mood. Ouch. No one wants to feel like this. Nor is it ever healthy to feel like this. Feeling this way will not lead you to become a 'better candidate' or increase your success of getting onto the clinical doctorate training. Feeling this way only costs your mental wellbeing, time, and energy.

○ ***Not all information for your clinical doctorate training application form is useful.*** Don't get me wrong, there will be times when the information provided feels relevant and will help you think about your career progression in a new light; however, this is not always the case. More often than not you will hear the same narrative churned out time and time again with respect to 'how to become a clinical psychologist' and it becomes stale. Sometimes the information is lacking as it misses significant characteristics which would be 'given standards' relevant to this career. Examples may be the omission of important terms and phrases (such as collaborative working and evidence-based research) when discussing application forms. In some cases, I have witnessed other assistant psychologists indicating you 'do not need to include such terms in your application form', advocate its omission. As you could imagine, such information is unhelpful and a hindrance to your development. If you were new to this line of work and had little support otherwise outside the group, you may be vulnerable to such misinformation. A part of me wondered whether assistant psychologists advocating such nonsense are in the game of deception, happily tripping up other people in order to succeed themselves. Perhaps I am just developing a conspiracy theory, or perhaps not...

The toxic psychology forum

Who has been on this online forum? Remember I told you to back away from it? I bet some of you ignored me and went back on the psychology forums to see what other people wrote. You say you do this, "in case it helps... I might learn something... I might get support". Complete BS. But it is your choice and apparently your brain cells directed you to go on the forum so, congratulations to your lack of self-control and need for external and truly meaningless assurance. I know, I sound harsh. Like I said at the start of this book – I am not filtering the reality of what is going on, just being honest.

Those psychology forums can be incredibly toxic. Imagine a place where all the competitive people come to meet. All of these people fighting to win the race and are happy enough to trip up anyone who gets in their way. Remember undergraduate psychology on anonymity mentality, that people are more likely to be aggressive and show unpleasant sides of themselves when they are anonymous and unreachable. Well you've just entered a forum of the anonymous aggressive assistant psychologists. Why? You allowed yourself to enter a place where you can be actively shot down by others. Even if you are standing on the side lines not engaging in active conversation, you observe how 'amazing' other people are doing which leaves you feeling bad about yourself. Whichever way it goes, you get destroyed in the process and you've volunteered yourself to be destroyed.

Many people who are competitive and secretive about their great application form can't help themselves but go on these forums. Yes, that includes the assistant psychologist I previously spoke about. She believed she could get helpful tips from these forums. Although there may be the rare helpful comment in these forums, they generally are filled with people displaying themselves as martyrs for the profession, fighting for what's right, and they believe they are the true and worthy applicants. There are even individuals who have clearly spent so much time and effort in other creative senses displaying 'how much they deserve' this by writing lengthy songs or poems and posting it on the forum. If you are spending so much time and energy writing songs and poems onto these forums, maybe you should redirect that energy to something, I don't know, useful? I recall someone I worked with who used to go on these forums commented that someone had posted they had applied for 13 years in a row and have not got onto the clinical doctorate training. Pal, if you have been applying for that number of years then clearly something is not working. Maybe you should stop, re-evaluate your life, and consider what would be most helpful for you with respect to your wellbeing and sanity. Maybe you need help in this process to support you in your reflections so that you can progress with your life in a healthy direction. Being stuck in time is clearly unhealthy and serves no one, and unfortunately it is you who suffers the most as a consequence. I would really like these people to get off their computer screen and realise that there is something more out there in their world and these forums are generally unhelpful. You can disagree with me as much as you want about this, but I am just telling you the truth. Perhaps it is time for you to get off your carriage of denial and face reality.

I know I can sound harsh but this is coming from a place of wanting you to focus on what is most helpful for yourself. This is you and only you. You are your own vehicle to success and regardless of how other people are performing. How other people are does not take away anything from you or make you any less. It does not eliminate your positive qualities or skills. It does not mean you are less worthy when you see other people who appear to be 'succeeding'. Allowing yourself to be absorbed in others' toxicity simply creates an environment wherein you become vulnerable and your risk of being hurt magnifies. My advice is to avoid such forums particularly during a time when you may already be stressed applying for the clinical training.

Principle 22
Never lose sight of your own as well as other people's maturity.

Principle 23
Develop the wisdom to notice the people around you; keep the people who support you close and distance those who damage you.

CHAPTER 13
Applying for the clinical doctorate training

"The cave you fear to enter holds the treasure you seek", Joseph Campbell.

Fear, fear, and more fear

If this book had sound effects, I would insert the music of the film Jaws. Since I can't do that and I imagine I would have to seek permission from the owners, I ask you to imagine the sound track. Just humour me.

Everyone applying for the clinical doctorate training experiences a range of feelings: distress, sadness, anxiety, fear, agitation, irritability, frustration, anger, and exhaustion. I am certain there are other emotions that I have not included in this list, but on the whole, there are many difficult experiences people have during this period of time. People initially look at the form, the sections they are required to complete alongside the limited number of characteristics they can show off their great attributes. This form really tests your ability to write in a concise way. Funny since all the way through formal education you are told to write essays that have to be thousands and thousands of words long, whereas now, when the time really matters, you need to express everything you are in a few short sentences. Another example of how education does not necessarily teach you skills you need to implement in real life, but I guess this is something someone else can comment on.

The difficult emotions experienced when facing and completing this application form stem from the fear of failure and having to wait another full year to apply again – only to potentially face another round of rejection. Basic instincts of fight or flight consume us as we see forms that are successful as reflecting survival of the fittest (psychologist). It is a natural reaction to experience this level of anxiety and fear when applying for the clinical doctorate training, because the reality is that the field is extremely competitive, and chances of success are low. People who succeed do have to work hard and demonstrate they have the right skills and personal qualities.

We can understand that these emotional responses are a natural reaction to the situation; however, it does not stop us from experiencing distress nor does it cause us to behave in certain ways. Our emotions, as much as our thoughts, can push us to do certain things and our bodies to respond in certain ways. I hope that you are able to notice such difficult feelings triggered during this process and find strength to let go of distress so that you can progress to a better stage of your life. "I learned that courage was not the absence of fear, but the triumph over it. The brave man is not he who does not feel afraid, but he who conquers that fear", Nelson Mandela.

The competitive streak is back in full force

Remember the earlier chapter where I spoke about the competitive assistant psychologists? This circumstance is certainly no exception – if anything, this is when their competitive side comes out to play the most. I appreciate this may come from a difficult sense that they are not good enough and wish to prove themselves, wish to be validated, and wish to be accepted. To be facing a very real and objectively challenging situation – to be selected out of thousands of applicants – is frightening and does instil the sense of smallness in you. People end up fighting their way through the crowd in the hope of being 'on top'.

When I was an assistant psychologist I worked closely with another assistant and she was applying for the clinical doctorate training course. She spent most of her working days on the computer, covering her screen with "work" whenever our supervisor walked in and as soon as our supervisor walked out she would quickly reverted back to revising her application form. Although I was not even applying that year, I remember her being very secretive that she was working on her application form. She would even shut down her application form whenever she got the sense that I entered the room or turned around to speak to her. It was almost as though she was concerned I would steal information from her amazing form and use it myself for when I did apply. Well, she clearly didn't know me that well. Even if I wanted to do that, which, let us be honest I have very little motivation or time for such garbage, I would not even have the mental capacity or ability to remember what it was she wrote. Nonetheless, she was very vigilant that no one saw her precious application form in case someone copied it. Interestingly though, she had no issue asking other assistant psychologists what they wrote on their application forms, how they broached certain sections, and how they would phrase certain statements. She would ask others to share their application forms with her, and some complied. Those who engaged in this conversation with her were quite open about their forms, about their work, and had a desire to help. I don't necessarily have an issue with people sharing their application forms with one another if they are both consenting to the process, but only if the individuals involved have the intelligence and due diligence to focus on their own work and identify what is appropriate and remain true to themselves and their experience. Unfortunately, this may not always happen as people who are operating from a place of fear may do unethical things like copying sentences and phrases from other people's application forms. P.S., this shows when universities come to read your forms, so please don't bother doing this.

Writing the form

Writing the form is a difficult process as there is no 'perfect' way of writing it that guarantees you an interview. There is no magic formulae or sequence of words you can use that will mean you will stand out among the thousands of applicants. People spend so much time and energy writing and re-writing their form, revising the details again and again to ensure it is as perfect as can be. Many people view this as a one shot opportunity to progress onto the career ladder. Although it is 'one shot a year' and not a lifetime, the process is a laborious one and thus it makes sense people are meticulous when completing the form. No one wants to go through that process again. Ever.

Most people do need one or two practice rounds of completing the form and going through the process simply to test the waters and identify how assessors respond to their application form in order to adjust and tweak it for the following year. Although there is no magic way of getting onto the course, there are certainly a few steps you can take to help you in the process.

- **Sources of professional support**. Identify people you know in a professional sense who are approachable and competent. Typically for many people, this would be their clinical supervisor though it may be another professional with whom you work and whose work you. In any case, ideally this individual is a clinical psychologist, someone who is further ahead on the career path. These individuals would be aware of the application process and can recognise what is important to document in your application form. I would suggest that you seek them for advice, discuss your work experience to date and they may help you flesh this out more, identify crucial points to discuss, and irrelevant areas you could discard. This person can help coach you and mentor you through the application process as well as the interview stage. Furthermore, ensure it is someone whom you trust and feel emotionally safe to share your experiences with, about this application process as well as your career in general. Experiencing such emotional safety will allow this process to feel easier and better, especially under anxiety provoking circumstances. Psychological studies have taught us people perform worse when feeling highly anxious and perform better when feeling safe and soothed. This suggests that in order to write an application form that reflects the best versions of ourselves, we need to feel safe and secure, and thus be surrounded by someone who helps us feel this way. You may be lucky enough to feel this way with your clinical supervisor, but if not, you can always approach another professional and that is perfectly fine. When I was applying for the course, I sought advice from a qualified clinical psychologist who was not my supervisor though she was in the same service. I had a lot of respect and admiration for this individual and I was grateful to have her support. Equally, I have also supported assistant psychologists I was not supervising in their application forms. The most helpful guidance and support you can receive is from someone whom you feel is competent and containing. This again reiterates my point earlier in this chapter, why would you seek advice from someone who is struggling themselves on the psychology forum?

- **Sources of personal and emotional support**. This too is important. Ideally the person you seek support from is someone whom you identify as emotionally available, consistent, and containing. It needs to be someone whom you trust. If this person is in the world of psychology, ideally they are at a different stage of their career from you. This is so that you both do not feed into each other's stress and anxieties as this could happen if you are both applying for the clinical training at the same time. This might just push you over the edge. Your source of emotional support needs to be stable during the time you are applying for the clinical training. It is also important this person has the capacity to provide you with that support. A friend who was applying for the clinical doctorate training sought emotional support from me while I was on the training course. Understandably, the application process was difficult for her and her anxiety quickly heightened when feeling insecure in her abilities. Luckily, I was at a different stage in my career and therefore from my end it was possible to provide containment and security, and she was able to receive this. Be mindful and choose wisely from the people you know who have the capacity to provide emotional support, even if this is not someone who you would usually seek support from. If you choose someone who has limited (or no) capacity to provide emotional security and safety, you may risk feeling rejected, vulnerable, and more distressed.

- **Be genuine**. You all probably heard this one and brushed it off, "yeah right, but really what do I write?". I am not saying be genuine to give you some airy fairy advice. It is true. There are so many application forms that look identical. All the same terminology and buzz words are used and therefore none of them stand out. Writing about how 'holistic' and 'person-centred' your approach is like writing about how water is wet. Everyone knows that this is important and states the same thing. Write about something that is genuine and personal to you. Why do you even want to become a clinical psychologist? What intimate and personal experiences do you have that drive you to this line of work? This may take some introspection to really delve deep and connect to why this really matters. I would highly advise you spend time doing this. As an example, for me it was around personally witnessing the longevity of power-imbalances stemming from abuse and consequential destructive relationships. It was around how some cultures dismiss the concept of mental health, have a different and potentially harmful interpretation of it, and how degrading and blaming this can feel. The more you are able to consider what it is about the field of mental health that fascinates you and draws you in, the more genuine you seem about your career (rather than being in it for the title), and the more your application form will stand out.

- **Be human and be balanced**. There will come a time when this application form dominates your world. You will feel there is nothing else that matters in the world other than this form. You will think about this form every minute of every day regardless of what you are doing. Your life will revolve around this application form. You may even sacrifice time in the shower, time eating, or time sleeping because you feel this is precious time that should be spent working on your form. Cutting down on the extra few seconds you spend under the shower to work on your form will not make the slightest bit of difference. If you cut back on your sleep, you will struggle to think clearly and become more likely to make mistakes. Surely you all must know this on a logical level. However, I have seen people going to such lengths thinking that this is going to help them in some way. I want to call this stupid but that might seem nasty. As a human being, we have basic needs as documented in Maslow's hierarchy of needs. Eating, sleeping, and being physically healthy are some of these. This means that we have to do activities in order to meet these needs so that we are able to accomplish more higher-level and complex activities. You may be saving 39 minutes over a month by missing showers and skipping meals here and there, but then you are beginning to neglect your basic needs. I previously talked about self-sacrifice in this book and although it may seem like the appropriate thing at the time as you are working towards a 'higher goal', it simply destroys your soul and wellbeing in the process. If you are not ok and the foundation is shaky, this process is going to be significantly shakier. Please ensure you are maintaining your own physical and psychological wellbeing in this process. This application is not the be all and end all of life. There are greater things out there. You do have a life outside of this career – and if you feel you do not, then please find one. Continue eating healthily, exercising, seeing friends, and sleeping well. Do not sacrifice your baser needs as this only serves to harm you.

Principle 24
Never allow the toxicity of others enter your heart

Principle 25
We can only grow successfully if we are feeling safe, secure, and soothed. Never lose sight of your basic needs as a human being, otherwise nothing else matters.

CHAPTER 14
The clinical doctorate training interview

"With peaks of joy and valleys of heartache, life is a roller coaster ride... It is both scary and exciting at the same time", Sebastian Cole.

Receiving a notification informing you of an interview for the clinical doctorate training brings on another rollercoaster of emotions. You have waited so long since you submitted your form that a part of you almost forgot about the process as you returned to your regular way of living. But now, you are called back into the boxing ring to fight for your survival. Having an interview may fill you with joy and excitement as you are getting ever closer to becoming qualified as a clinical psychologist. This might also fill you with anxiety and fear as you realise that the game is on. You must prepare for this moment which will determine your future career progression. The opportunity is limited so you must give it your best shot. During this time, you may also discover that you got interviews that other assistant psychologists that you worked with did not, and vice versa. This may bring a sense of jealousy, sadness, shame, anger, anxiety, sadness, and commiserations. The competition continues as you face the reality that only the best of the best would get interviews, and thus the standards are raised once again. If and when you can, let go of the difficult emotions that do not serve you and refocus your energy on what you can control, what you can do, and how you can move forward in this situation.

Preparing for the interview

Now you have gotten over your panic knowing you will have an interview for the clinical training, take a few deep belly breaths and collect your thoughts.

Each university seems to have a different interview procedure. Some universities have a short and intense 30 minute interview, others have a day full of one-to-one and group interviews along with presentations and tests. The style of interview is inconsistent across the board, which in itself is challenging as the ideal way of preparing for the interview becomes unclear. Furthermore, the processes that each university follows changes year on year, meaning it can become even trickier to prepare as you may be faced with an unexpected task the university decided to add in the year you have an interview. I can feel the joy resonating from your aura.

As daunting as the interviews seem, there are a few things you can do to prepare and strengthen your confidence.

- **Find out the structure of the interview**. The first and most simple step. Find out what type of interview the university has and whether this has changed from previous years. Knowing whether it is a full day or a brief interview will give you a sense of what you need to do to prepare.

- **Find someone who has had that interview**. By this I mean find a qualified clinical psychologist who had an interview at the same university. Ask them for advice with respect to what the interview was like, what types of questions they ask, what topics they explore, and how best to present responses.

- **Revise both clinical and research matters**.
  - Some of us may be more clinically oriented while others are more research oriented. To succeed at this interview, you need to demonstrate that you are competent at both and have the ability to develop skills in both. Learn clinically relevant models and consider all aspects of your clinical work; what you would do with a service user from start to finish. This may be assessment, formulation, intervention, and evaluation of intervention as well as managing risk, identifying personal goals, involving the multidisciplinary team, societal and cultural factors, and unidentified needs. To help you consolidate your learning, you may apply such questions to case studies that you find online, in books, or service users using certain models like CBT or Attachment Theory. Think about different clinical tools you may use to measure symptoms and evaluate the

effectiveness of the therapy. It is perfectly acceptable to learn a couple of models and tools really well that can be applied across many different clinical presentations or problems (otherwise known as 'transdiagnostic') so that they can be adapted to different cases. Like I mentioned earlier in the book, it is better to learn a couple of models extremely well so that you are able to thoroughly discuss them and justify their use at interview, rather than lots of models in brief or inadequate detail (and due to time constraints, you may not be able to show off how many models you have learnt). Display the depth of knowledge you have as well as precision around your work. Consider the best cases you have worked with clinically, cases of which you are most proud, and why they were such a success. Think of elements you can extract from these that can be adopted in the interview.

o   Do not forget about research methods. Not only do I mean learn the difference between qualitative and quantitative research, but really think about different forms of qualitative and quantitative research; the types of research questions they are designed for, their pros and cons, and the reality of applying this research method. Given any study type, consider why you might choose one research methodology over another and your justification for this choice. In the weeks leading up to interviews, I developed a large revision folder filled with lots of information on different research methods. I went over these notes again and again, writing about them in different ways to ensure I really understood them. Again, you are only going to get good at research methods if you go through example research questions and map out possible research methods, following through from beginning to end as to how this research would transpire.

-   For both clinical and research examples, practice, practice, and practice again till you are bored of it. That is when you know you understand the information and you are able to apply it to any given case study.

- **Practice interviews**. Find a qualified clinical psychologist, preferably someone who has had an interview at the same university and ask them to do a mock interview with you. They can give you a sense of the types of questions asked, the attitudes of the examiners, and critique your responses. Luckily, my clinical supervisor at the time had an interview at the same university and so she supported me to practice with a mock interview. I knew it was a mock situation and thus it should not have been anxiety provoking but weirdly it was. It provided me with a sense of how some of the questions would be structured, how I should structure my responses, and how the interviewers might respond to me. The more mock interviews you are able to do, the better as you will become more confident and less anxious about the process. If the psychologist who does the mock interview with you succeeded with an offer at that university then great and follow their recommendations. If they did not get offered a place, learn from their reflections as to what would have helped them succeed.

- **Do whatever soothes and regulates you**. Among all the chaos, you will have to find a way to regulate your own emotions and engage in something that relieves stress and supports your wellbeing. This is the only way you are going to maintain your sanity in this stressful situation as well as improve your ability to prepare and perform at the interview. This may be meditation, yoga, socialising, reading, watching tv, painting, or hardcore exercise. Along with this, ensure your basic needs are met. I said earlier if our basic physical and psychological needs are denied, everything comes tumbling down particularly under such circumstances.

The interview itself

The day has come. You have not been able to sleep the night before (or perhaps the last 2 weeks) as your anxiety has hit the roof. What do you do?

- **Be professional.** Like so many things this should be blatantly obvious, but it goes amiss for some people. I am referring to the language you use, your attitude, and the clothes that you wear. This is a simple point but weirdly some people think that this is not necessary and they are able to either 'kick it' with interviewers or 'sway' the interviewers in some way. For instance, there have been a string of girls over the years who have attended the interviews and attempted to seduce male interviewers by wearing a low cut-top and short skirt with bare legs. I know some people would bombard me with this remark I just made– get off your high horse and calm down, I am a feminist and I understand such clothes should not be viewed as an 'invitation'. Frankly though, in these circumstances sexual seduction is the intention of the interviewee. This does not work; interviewers know you are doing this and it is viewed as incredibly inappropriate – even if you are a perfectly good candidate, they would likely decline you based on such unprofessionalism. Would you be turning up to work in such provocative clothing? Hopefully not when working with vulnerable people. Other points would be making sure your phone is turned off, ensure you have all relevant documents, and that you turn up on time.

- **Pause and think.** At times when we become so anxious, effective communication can become really difficult. We may find that words escape us, or we might end up talking too fast. Either way, we feel as though we are not presenting the best version of ourselves or the best knowledge we have. It is perfectly acceptable to pause and think about the response you are going to construct. It may feel like eternity in your mind during that moment, but objectively it is not that long. Having those few extra seconds to consider your response will help you provide a much better response in the manner you wish to present yourself. There is no need to rush, the situation is pressurising enough as it is. Take a deep breath and think.

- **Human errors happen, acknowledge them and do not be ignorant.** We are all human, we all make mistakes. This can also happen in the interview, and the type of mistake we make can vary – for instance it may be from muddling up our words or not having the appropriate item on us. For example, I recall I mistakenly used the word "systematic" when I actually meant to say "systemic"; luckily, I quickly corrected myself and that was fine. Another individual I know of had to engage the board in a presentation, but he could not find his memory stick that contained his presentation. Extremely unfortunate. He acknowledged his error and powered through with printouts he had previously made. He was successful in getting accepted onto the training course. The interviewers are humans and recognise that candidates are human as well. We all make errors and that is normal. How we manage these errors provides the interviewers with insight as to how we would manage challenges in the real world. Interviewers would like to see that we are able to acknowledge difficulties and we can problem solve these in ways that are appropriate. Handling such situations in ways that displays competency indicates acceptability of error. What is unacceptable is being ignorant or ignoring errors, pretending like they are not there. For example, I have heard of people accidentally leaving their phone on loud and receiving a call during the interview. There might have been an awkward ring tone like NSync's Bye Bye Bye, but the individual ignored the fact their phone was ringing and pretended like it was not happening, continuing to answer the interview questions. I would like to know, what impression did this person think the interviewers had of them in that moment? Everyone could clearly hear it. Again, such an event is human error, unfortunate but natural. Recognise, apologise, and move on appropriately. Not doing so just makes you look ignorant.

- **If you do not know the answer, reflect on this**. At any point in our stage of development, there will be areas which we do not know or understand. Course directors and tutors are aware of this, and the purpose of the clinical doctorate training is to ensure everyone who qualifies develops to the same clinical and research level. If your knowledge and experience is significantly lacking, then perhaps you should reconsider and apply the following year (though it is unlikely you would be called for an interview if you were at this stage). However, if you are in the interview and there is a question or sub-question where you are unsure of the answer, it is ok to say this. The crucial part here is to comment on how you would discover the answer to this information. In my interview, there was a question on a clinical case study to which I was unsure what the 'correct' response was. The question was "what is this person's goals". I remember scrambling around attempting to remember the case study and specific details included. However, I was genuinely unsure what the right answer was. My response reflected this. I commented that "it could be x, y, z as these were elements included in the case study, but I honestly don't know for sure because the service user has not explicitly stated what his goals were. I can only really find out by asking the person". Soon after this I received a letter of acceptance to the university. Interviewers appreciate honesty as well as seeing the process you would undertake in real life. Interviewers know that even when you qualify you will not know the answer to everything so quit pretending like you do now. Doing so can lead to missing out on crucial information and further incompetency.

- **Be human.** At one point during my interview, I dropped formalities and I showed myself fully. It was at a point when I got asked the question, "what would I do if I saw a service user who was not ok". I mentioned I would check out risk, identify protective factors, explore the context etc. but then, I remember going out on a limb and I went on to speak about what is the point of having mental health services if healthcare professionals were not going to show service users care and respect. I then spoke about how I would offer them tea and biscuits, engage them in an activity such as pool, and how I would just want to have a normal conversation with them about anything. After this, my heart dropped as I quickly re-orientated myself back to the room and remembered who was in front of me. I regretted talking about how great chocolate digestive biscuits were. Strangely though, this answer worked. It showed that I was human, I had a compassionate and empathic side, that I would do what I could to improve the person's wellbeing and that I had the desire to spend time with them, to show them I valued them, and that I wanted to connect to them. This was important for the service user who was interviewing to hear, and by the way, they are the most important individual who is interviewing – not the clinical directors and professors.

Oh the tears. This entire process is an emotionally straining time. It is horrific to go through and your friends and family who have not been through it may not appreciate the magnitude of stress you experience. Some of you may cry and that is ok. In fact, some research shows that crying may be helpful in re-establishing the homeostatic balance of electrons in your body and supporting the release of endorphins. But perhaps don't cry during the interview, try to hold it till after the interview. This is simply to give yourself the opportunity to provide the best responses you can during the interview, display that you are competent and capable of tolerating stressful situations (and believe me there is a lot more stress where you're going). After my interview, I cried for about 12 hours straight. No joke. Luckily, I had taken the following day off as annual leave. If you think you might feel sensitive afterwards, I advise you do the same – give yourself a break away from work. Find a way you can relax and take your mind away from the nightmare of getting onto the course.

Principle 26
"Give me six hours to chop down a tree and I will spend the first four sharpening the axe", Abraham Lincoln.
Preparation and rehearsal is key to developing confidence and ensuring your best chances.

Principle 27
"The truest story − the one that will always be truest − is that I am a human being, being human. Sometimes, I am my best self. Sometimes, not so much. I am trying to do better... My guess is that you are, too", Laura McKowen.
Be honest and true to yourself; from this self-reflection can grow.

CHAPTER 15
Dealing with rejection from the clinical doctorate training programme

"Failure is not the opposite of success; it's part of success", Arianna Huffington.

"You cannot achieve success without the risk of failure, and I learned a long time ago you cannot achieve success if you fear failure", Paul Heyman.

Not getting an interview

Unfortunately, some people are not invited to an interview, even when they have the right clinical and research skills as well as personal qualities. How do you deal with this? Well, I knew one girl who did not get an interview and boy did she give the professor on the selection panel a hard time. This girl approached the professor and berated him for the university not selecting her for interview. She argued that she 'did everything' stated as a requirement for interview and it was a worldly injustice that she did not get selected. Watching this, I was a little concerned that she may go ahead and punch him. This is a fantastic example of how you should not respond. I can appreciate that her response came from a place of anger, frustration, and overall sense of unfairness; however, it certainly did not help her. It is horrific getting rejected, it triggers a sense of being subpar and regardless of how hard you work, you are not good enough. No one wants to feel this way. It also reinforces the sense of helplessness while others (i.e. 'the course') hold ultimate power for our future. You may find yourself trying to job hunt again as your temporary contract is coming to an end and you do not have any financial security. All of these experiences are extremely difficult. But becoming aggressive and irate with another individual (particularly course directors) as well as expressing your BS entitlement is just unacceptable. You can spend time crying, screaming into a pillow, calling your friends to complain. Do whatever you need to do to regulate your emotions so that you can feel emotionally safe and settled again. Then when you are ready, you can review your form and work out what you may have missed out on and areas you can improve. You may do this when you are reapplying the following year so as to give yourself some headspace and allow time to pass so that you have developed further experience. As stated in the motto of Acceptance and Commitment Therapy: have the wisdom to know what you can control and accept what you cannot change. Focus on would be most helpful for you at this time.

Rejection following the interview

As I mentioned, being rejected is awful. Rejection following the interview may fill you with the sense of "so close, yet so far". This may fill us with dread, thinking we will have to go through the process all over again the following year. Again, do what you need to do to regulate your emotions, to find emotional safety. Recognise that this course is not your entire life – you have things in your life beyond the course that are irreplaceable, such as family and friends. Of course, your career is important, but this clinical training course is not the be all and end all. Do not be like one of those trolls on the psychology forums talking about how not getting on the course is going to end their life. If you honestly believe that your life is over if you do not get on it, please seek help. Seek professional help. Seek support from friends and clinical supervisors and when you are ready, you can review what happened and how you can improve. We are all on this challenging journey. Remember the message Plato shared with the world; upmost respect and admiration goes to those who make efforts in the attempt to better themselves. These people will be the ones who succeed.

Principle 28
"Success is not final, failure is not fata: it is the courage to continue that counts", Winston Churchill.

CHAPTER 16
I got on the clinical doctorate training!

"A dream doesn't become reality through magic; it takes sweat, determination and hard work", Colin Powell.

Welcome to Hogwarts. Getting onto the clinical doctorate training is like being able to find your entry to platform $9^{3/4}$ – we all know it is a fictional place reserved for the special few. It is hidden and you are seen as odd by other people as you repeatedly run into that brick wall only to get knocked back to reality. See the resemblance? There are plenty, I could go on. This journey of the clinical training course is full of ups and downs. Times you see your supervisor taking off their wig and you realise they are two faced. Times the shy person in class astonishes you. Times you will be grateful for having survived the three headed monster aka: clinical work, lectures, and thesis. I only just learnt about Harry Potter in 2019 (I watched 2 of the films if you care), and I was smacked in the face by metaphors of how these films related to the course.

Settle in, your journey to train as a clinical psychologist is about to begin.

Phase 1: Starting the course

Many of the courses have an 'introduction social event' before the commencement of the training itself. This is an opportunity for you to meet your cohort in a relaxed social setting so that you can begin to know one another. Some courses just have a food and drink evening while other courses go all out and have you doing a full activity day together. Either way, I would recommend that you go on this social event if possible. It is a nice way of getting to know each other while everyone is friendly, content, and relaxed before they start getting on your nerves as the course intensifies.

"Drink some coffee and pretend you know what you are doing", author unknown. You turn up to the course induction at the university. Some of you may have decided it was a good idea to spend 3 hours deliberating over which pencil case and note pad you would like to buy because it's cute and will definitely make you work better while people like me won't even turn up with a bic pen, but most definitely with a coffee in hand. Like the first day of school, you have butterflies in your stomach. You experience a mix of emotions and thoughts; anxieties around how the training will transpire, how you will get on with other people, excitement that you finally cracked your way onto the clinical training, and relief that you don't have to be concerned about applying for jobs for the next 3 years.

During the introduction phase of the course, like any new job or NHS Trust induction, you will not learn a lot except for who are the best people to sit next to in class, which tutor has the drollest voice, and that prejudice and discrimination almost always exist. That little bubble you may have had that the course is filled with "progressive thinkers because we are all psychologists" may get a tiny pinprick. Sorry guys. Typically, this actually comes from those who are teaching / inducting students rather than the students themselves which at least provides a ray of hope as younger generations can support helpful future change. What I am about to note as an example of prejudice may be inappropriate to write in this book however I feel silence would be permitting prejudice to occur. I recall in the first week of induction, a senior member of staff from the associated NHS Trust had visited to speak to us about how the Trust functioned and its structure. Along with this what was seemingly an appropriate topic, she (remember 'she') noted, "this course is extremely stressful and you will be busy, so I do not advise you to get pregnant". Hmm. Well that is interesting to hear. This statement shocked many of us. I suspect part of her reasoning was that having women going on maternity leave would be 'too costly' for the Trust particularly during training and so... better to ensure people do not choose having a family over work?! The previous academic cohort had many people on maternity leave which may have provoked her to make this comment as well. Although parts of that statement are true, the course can be stressful and you will be busy, if you want to have a family that is your choice and it is perfectly ok. Do not have some random person who does not know you telling you what to do with your life. Remember this statement throughout your entire journey: *the course is not your life; your life is much greater and so it should be.* I sincerely hope that no one else experiences this and that you are all welcomed onto the course for who you are and for your life choices. Overall you will note that your classmates come from different backgrounds and have experiences and personal values. Having said that, there are times when the entire cohort is full of young, Caucasian, middle-class women so... swings and roundabouts. Arguments around equality and fair representation go beyond this book but, it is something to hold in mind.

During the initial few weeks, you will meet your academic and your clinical tutors. Hope they are nice and friendly! For the most part they will be, though just a pre-warning the tutors are humans and as human beings, they may have particular interaction styles that are suited or misaligned to yours. The way that your tutor initially interacts with you may provide you with great insight into their relationship styles and how supportive they will be of you through your journey. Just as an example, I emailed my academic tutor in the first week to arrange an introductory meeting. Meeting arranged, I went to see him and waited outside his office. I suspect he forgot about who I was / who he was meeting. As he walked into his office, we laid eyes on each other for the first time. I asked, "are you X [first name]". He very quickly responded with a firm, "I am Dr X [surname]", as if to suggest I was not allowed to call him by his first name. Wow check out the power imbalance here. Can't imagine he would have been the most therapeutic with service users, though I could be wrong. Feeling as small as a peanut I apologised for assuming it was ok to call him by his first name and I explained who I was. The embarrassment on his face was clear as daylight as he recognised that he behaved arrogantly. Laughably his justification was, "sorry I thought you were an undergraduate student, of course you can call me X [first name]". So, what if I was an undergraduate student? Doesn't make me any less important as a human being, does it? But again, this demonstrates the illusion that people on the clinical doctorate training are somehow 'special'. Jeepers Creepers, not sure how much I wanted to be part of the elite if the elite are arrogant. Like the beautiful Tom Hardy said, "I was raised to treat the janitor with the same respect as the CEO"; and it should be. Unfortunately, this is representative of how you may be belittled throughout your career, an embryonic symbol of further battles around your 'worth' as you progress. No wonder the whole process of trying to qualify as a clinical psychologist feels like you are perpetually being stabbed in the heart, and the face. Experiencing this, I thought it must be frightening being a service user, fearing the superiority of professionals, and that you would be whipped if you ever thought you could be on the same level as another human being. Disgraceful.

Now I have given you hope about the journey you are about to embark upon filled with unicorns and rainbows, sit back and relax (perhaps by watching comedy on your smart phone during lectures).

Principle 29
It's exciting and it's scary. But never lose sight of what really matters to you.

CHAPTER 17
Lectures on a new (yet old) level

"We are shut up in schools and college recitation rooms for ten or fifteen years and come out at last with a bellyful of words and do not know a thing", Ralph Waldo Emerson.

People entering clinical training come from different occupational backgrounds, developing experience in certain clinical and research settings, meaning that each individual may have great knowledge in specific areas and lack knowledge in others. The purpose of the clinical training is to ensure that everyone qualifies with the same level of clinical, research, and academic competency and knowledge. The focus or orientation of the teaching may vary across different universities; for instance, some courses may be focused more on relational approaches while others may be more CBT focused. Either way, the courses generally provide lectures in the same major subjects to ensure standardisation and this is reviewed year after year with other universities, reviewed against national British Psychological Society's standards.

The lectures are designed to teach, provoke thought, and support the link between the evidence base and clinical practice. Learning styles may vary between students and thus opinions on the lectures can differ across the board. Equally, the lectures provided can vary in terms of content, depth, and style dependant on the individual delivering the lecture. Personally, I prefer lectures that are more conversational based involving activities, especially role plays (many people cringe at that last part). Research suggests learning is often consolidated by putting it into practice rather than simply being a passive participant aka listening with the information going in one ear, it will soon come out the other. Anyone can sit there quietly and do nothing. Look around you, even walls do that. I know for most of my educational life, including many of yours, this is exactly what you do during lectures. And for many of you, sitting quietly in response to questions asked by the lecturer in the attempt to elicit a discussion is the common response. Egh that silence is uncomfortable. Why are you dragging it out? Everyone on the clinical doctorate training has been in lectures before, though typically these lectures have taken a different form whereby over 100 students may be present and therefore class discussions are infrequent. The purpose of lectures at clinical training level is entirely different: its purpose is to be applied to real life clinical situations, to have valid meaning, and to influence someone's life. Becoming a more active participant during class is imperative if you want to become any good. Putting yourself out there and accepting the risk that you may make mistakes indeed requires courage and this will help you strengthen your skills and confidence in becoming a much better clinician and researcher. If you are able to put the messages of the lecture into practice during the lecture then great, if you are able to put it into practice in a clinical setting then even better. Some of the lectures may appear more relevant than others and their relevance may fluctuate dependent on the stage of the course. Nonetheless I would encourage you all to hold in mind elements of each topic area as many of the teachings will be applicable across different presentations and settings; they are often transdiagnostic and transtherapeutic.

-   **In one ear and out the other:** "Education gets in the way of my learning", Mark Twain. "We shouldn't teach great books, we should teach a love of reading. Knowing the contents of a few works of literature is a trivial achievement. Being inclined to go on reading is a great achievement", B. F. Skinner. As you may have gathered in previous chapters, I am not the biggest fan of formal education. It is not necessarily the most helpful teacher, especially if its real life application is difficult. Unfortunately, many of the lecturers teaching clinical topics had been out of clinical practice for a long time. Already not a helpful start. Such lecturers may have somewhat gotten out of touch with what we find in current clinical practice; service users' difficulties and presentations may be different, complexity is the 'new norm', thresholds for services are heightened, and service users are more involved in their care. When teaching, the information is shared in such a way that it is incredibly difficult to conceptualise and / or understand how to implement it practically. It can feel very unhelpful for reasons outlined below:

- **Too simplistic.** "An investment in knowledge pays the best interest", Benjamin Franklin. Many of the lectures taught are about a specific clinical presentation or issue, demonstrated in a way that appears almost 'exclusive' of any other difficulty. For example, 'just depression' or 'just generalised anxiety disorder'. News flash: people don't 'just' have one diagnosis or difficulty. If you hadn't realised, people are complex. Furthermore, as societies progress, technology changes, new illnesses (e.g. COVID-19) transpire, and illicit substances are manufactured; people's experiences and problems are going to become more complex. Research everywhere suggests that comorbidity of psychological problems with the addition of socio and medical problems are often the norm rather than the exception – Google will show you thousands of pages confirming this. People who access services do not merely just have depression because they have 'thinking biases'. They have a lot more going on than that. And if we were to neglect the rest of their experiences we would be doing them a disservice. Thresholds to access mental health services are often increasing. This has been done in a way that is perhaps inadvertent. Back in the mid 2000's, mental health services got a lot of attention particularly because of the impact that mental health sickness had on the economical state of the UK. This led to the development of 'Improving Access to Psychological Therapies' (IAPT) services in 2008, and along with this came self-help services and computerised therapy programmes. Hallelujah our prayers have been answered! You have been so lonely for a long time, you felt that no one understood the emotional pain you have been through, and there was nothing to help. Well look no further, the government has the perfect solution for you: a computer bot. Brilliant! This pre-programmed bot has all the responses you need, just ignore any irrelevant comments or examples it provides you with, allow it to test your patience till the end of the earth, and just remember don't self-harm because it is just a machine and can't call A&E for you. Sorry, please excuse my sarcasm while I shoot myself in the foot. In any case, this system means that those with 'just depression' or 'just anxiety' can go speak to the robot, while the more complex cases must be seen by people. We would hope these people are competent. Hope is the key word here. How do you manage such complexity, how do you sit with such difficulty, how do you personally emotionally respond to this, how does that influence your practice and the service user sat in front of you? Could you ever become competent based on these lectures? Or simply frightened when you are in practice faced with complexity, frantically searching through your 398 slides on nothing.

○ **Death by PowerPoint.** There will be times when you feel you are sat down for eternity listening to someone going through an endless number of slides. As you're clock watching and counting down the minutes till the grim reaper comes and puts an end to the lecture, your brain turns itself off and you shut down. Gazing to the front of the class, you realise you have just wasted a few hours of your life on which you cannot get a refund. When such lectures finish, you realise you weren't sure what topic you just got taught as the topic title noted on your academic calendar may not match up with what you have just sat through. So, like any good student wanting to develop my learning, I decided to go on YouTube and watch videos that explain the subject, preferably in an animation format. As much as it may have looked like I was just watching cartoons, I must say this has been the best form of education for me, hands down. This may not be the format in which other people learn I know, but it definitely beats 3 hours learning something that could be said in a few sentences. The reason I mention this is that there may be times you may have to search for an alternative method to consolidate (or even begin) your learning on a particular subject as the format of the lecture may be unsuitable. Helpfully though, not all lectures are death by PowerPoint. Some lectures actually get you to discuss the subject and engage in activities around the subject;

helping you learn by doing which is the best way of learning and retaining the information. Fingers crossed you have more of these types of lectures.

o **Research from long, long ago.** As I hear you all cheering and throwing your arms in the air like you just don't care, I'm going to ask you to settle down while we learn about events occurring in the 17th Century. On occasion, you'll find lecturers referencing research that was completed many, many moons ago. The issue with this is that as much as it was valid for the time it was completed, societies change and so do the populations and potential clinical presentations / difficulties, as mentioned above. I know, I'm lazy too and sometimes I can't be bothered to do too much work and avoid it if possible, so I guess some lecturers may take the same approach and use the same exact slides as they did 10 years ago. However, things do change. Also, it's nice to be courteous to the students who are sat patiently, wanting to learn to develop their career by providing them something relevant.

o **Research, research, and more research.** "Hey, did you know that I'm really into research" said lecturer nobody. Sometimes, the subjects are taught primarily from a research perspective and there is little about anything else i.e. what do you actually do clinically. I don't want to scare you but in all honesty, but I don't think the lectures I had actually prepared me for real life clinical work. Lectures on really important topics such as trauma or dissociation (or even depression) were so theoretically driven that there was very little information on practical steps that you take when you have a service user in front of you. Of course, research is important as this evidences why we should / should not provide certain care, therapeutic approach, techniques etc. However, it is still necessary to discuss what actually needs to be done. What does the research actually mean in real terms? How can this be applied? And what about the cases where the research is not suggested? For you research and stats buffs, you may realise that in a way (a very sneaky way, shh don't tell), you can sometimes skew the results to make them show whatever you wanted to show? Obviously, this poses an ethical dilemma, though there is some truth within what I am saying. Given we work with people in clinical settings who are not research participants, what relevance does this research actually have? Research is rendered useless if it does not have any real life practical implications and discussions around how this would be applied, which is the best way to apply it, how do we know we are successful in its application, and how does it help service users. Learning about research from the people who actually conducted the studies themselves, speaking about the methodology and therapeutic techniques with demonstrations can allow us to learn so much more than just lines of names with dates. As I noted earlier, if you can put research into practice please do, that is the only real way of learning, understanding, and developing yourself professionally.

- ○ **Strict models vs. idiosyncratic**. A fun debate for all the family. Which model do you use and why? Some students, lecturers and clinicians are of the view that psychological models should be strictly adhered to when working with a service user while other people suggest that this is inappropriate as "humans don't fit into boxes". Might it depend on how big and malleable the box is? I'm not going to explicitly state which camp I tend to sit in, though what I will say is that both sides of the argument make sense. Using models that are evidenced in research is important as we have justification for the work we are doing, and thus should be adhered to as anything else may potentially be harmful or unhelpful. As the HCPC standards of conduct, performance, and ethics state: do no harm; and the research suggests this is the least harmful method with most potential benefits. However, people are complex, and service users rarely just have panic disorder or depression and thus how could we use a model that only targets one difficulty among a comorbidity of difficulties? Equally, many of the psychological models taught are very psycho, psycho, psycho while paying little attention to sociological and biological features which as we know play a significant part in our lives. Take a look at Maslow's hierarchy of needs – the foundation itself indicates we need shelter (sociological), food, water, and treatment of physical ailments (biological). If we do not include sociological and biological needs then what are we doing? The rest of our pyramid may very well collapse. As we work with service users in the real world, together we can explore and understand the individual, shape and reshape how the difficulties are viewed, and finding a helpful way to develop and grow.

Principle 30
Develop the wisdom to identify information that would be helpful for you to learn and have the willingness to think and learn independently to develop your own knowledge base from which you can grow.

Principle 31
Theory without practical relevance is meaningless, practice without theory is unwise.

CHAPTER 18
Exams

"Genius is 1% talent and 99% hard work", Albert Einstein.

Despite the stress that exams cause, they were created with the purpose of helping you learn. Although I'm not entirely sure how well that translates into the real world especially when it comes to the clinical doctorate course, I do believe there is some truth in that. Exams are not designed to catch you out but they are designed to examine the depth of your knowledge and how you are able to implement your knowledge in ways that are helpful, accurate, and thorough. People perceive exams differently, some people like exams and prefer these to doing assignments while other people despise exams and would rather complete other work. Either way, exams can be a stressful time and generally put you into a state of anxiety which is usually an unpleasant experience for anyone.

- **The early revisers**. Some people scarily start revising and reading research around the exam subject weeks if not months in advance, preparing early hoping this will provide them with an edge and guaranteed success. I am definitely not this type of person. I am the type who panics going through the lecture slides, books, and research papers about 1 or 2 weeks before the exam. I'm not saying either way is right or better. Hopefully by this stage in your academic life you will know which revision technique works best for you with respect to your knowledge and to your anxiety levels, whether that be revising with plenty of time or cramming it all in. In all fairness, there is evidence to support both methods of learning (see, I said you can skew research to get the results you want). Reasons for revising with plenty of time is that you are able to go over it time and again to process the information into your long-term memory banks and reduce anxieties around examination as you build your confidence. Revising with little time available can also be helpful as the time constraints force you to focus on what is important and relevant, blocking out white noise.

- **Method of revision**. Some people are thinkers, some people are doers, some people are visual, some people are verbal. Again, hopefully, you know which description best fits you, and if you need some help thinking about this you can revert back to an earlier chapter. However, do not worry if you're still unsure of your learning style. I definitely did not know which one best fit me. So, when it came to revising, I struggled to know which method would help me learn. I was hoping I would know which one I was so I could find the easy way of learning. As you can tell, I can get very lazy. But in all honestly, there probably isn't an easy way of learning, it requires hard work. And perhaps you just have to try out all the methods; throw it all on the wall and see which one sticks. In this way, I quickly realised which method did not suit me. I could then eliminate what I could not tolerate and focused on what felt more comfortable and easier.

- **Precise vs. broad**. Earlier in the book, the debate came up as to which is better – to learn a few subjects in depth, or many subjects as much as possible. After trying both methods, I was much more successful and far less stressed using the first approach. For my first couple of exams, I was so worried that I wouldn't do well so I tried my very best revising everything I could and gave myself plenty of time to do so. This was the only time when I actually spent around 6 weeks revising, rather than restricting my revision time as I previously mentioned. Fear was instilled in me when I was told that the exams were difficult to pass and there was a covert "3 strikes and you're out" rule. The rule essentially stated that if you fail 3 things over the 3 years of the course, then you would ultimately fail the entire thing and would not qualify. As it felt near enough impossible to get onto the course, I was not willing to take the chance of failing so early on in my journey – save that for times when I'm in real trouble. In my third year, there was some conversation that this rule was apparently untrue despite the definite undertone indicating it was. Perhaps the sense of this being true was designed to create so much fear in students that they are driven to revise and work hard throughout training. Feeling this fear, I decided to learn anything and everything my brain could possibly retain for the first couple of exams. Results: just at the pass mark, no more, bang on 50% which was the pass mark at the time. Really? I left the exams thinking I did reasonably well given how hard I worked, how much I wrote, and the breadth of knowledge I displayed. When it got to my second year of training, I began to get fed up with the course and my patience as well as motivation was wearing thin. Bombarded with even more exams, which we had to balance with more placement assignments and thesis work, I decided that less was more. I figured that I could only realistically revise so much before I wanted to gouge my eyes out with a fork. So, I essentially learnt one theory well and believed I could apply it to anything and everything I was presented with. If you're interested, it was (drum roll) attachment theory. Possibly not as exciting as you might have thought, but it is true. I chose this mainly because it was easy enough to learn and I could apply it to children, adults, older adults, whether they have a learning disability or are neuro atypical, families, relationships, therapeutic relationship and how to manage dynamics, relationship to their emotional difficulties, as well as how they view their physical health. This can leave you thinking about the function of certain presentations and how you develop healthier ways of being and thus reducing related distress. I generally believe you could use any psychological model and adapt it to most presentations and case studies you are presented with in an exam as long as you make sure of 2 things. 1) you choose a model that is transdiagnostic. 2) you practice creativity in its application. This way, it is far better to learn one or two models very well as you can think about this in a lot of detail and display this in your response, rather than showing you know a little about a lot wherein you can't go into too much detail. This approach is also better for maintaining your sanity throughout the process of revision because time to revise and your resources are finite; it would be extremely difficult to learn a lot about everything. When I took this narrow and detailed approach to revision, my pass marks significantly improved to 75-90%. Not saying this to show off but the proof is in the pudding.

- **Stress and sleep**. During the revision and exam period, you are probably going to experience a level of stress. Some people get very stressed while others find it easier. This can manifest itself in different ways and so it is important to be mindful of how you experience stress. Consider what it is that might happen to you which is unhealthy and unhelpful and if there is any way of protecting yourself from this and improving the situation. For instance, I know I eat a lot more when I'm stressed (I also generally just love food), I get more tired, and I struggle to sleep. Knowing this, I am aware it is also important to keep exercising regularly to make sure I burn off any extra cakes I'm eating and to wear myself out enough so that I get a good night's sleep. Doing this also ensures that I have a break away from revision and I have time that is truly just for me. I recommend you do the same, whether that be exercise, seeing friends, or watching your favourite TV series. Make sure you have a break from what feels like a dreadful time so that you can focus on yourself. As we know, when we feel anxious, tense, and low in mood we generally perform much worse than if we were feeling confident, calm, and relaxed. So, do whatever you need to ensure your wellbeing which we will talk about more later in this book. Many people like to celebrate the end of the exams by going out afterwards. Although I liked this idea I always struggled with the reality of it. At the exam when our body's natural fight or flight system has been activated, adrenaline and cortisol rushing around the body, I feel knackered and just want to sleep. It almost felt as though sleep was my 'celebration' signifying the end of the stressful period.

- **All bad, nothing good**. This really refers to the marker's comments on your exam paper. This may be different at different universities and courses, but I know for the most part, the examiners comment on everything you have done wrong and missed with very little acknowledgement or comments on what you have done right. This absolutely is true for people who pass. Therefore, logic would suggest that if my responses were good enough to pass, what was it I did right to have passed? Wouldn't that be important to know so I can keep whatever it was I did right and do more of it? Surely this is the basis of social learning theory and positive reinforcement, psychology 101. We also know that research suggests negative reinforcement or punishment may not work as well as positive reinforcement so... what's up examiners? Of course, it is important to know what I could improve on so I can enhance my skills and more importantly, enhance my knowledge. However, there is a helpful and unhelpful way of going about this to support someone else's learning. Lecturers are in the business of teaching and thus should be teaching in ways that are helpful. It may not be intentional, but the way the comments are written would often come across as critical and punitive which is certainly an unhelpful way of learning. Students who experience that emotional pain try their best to get rid of it and avoidance is the number 1 strategy to do so, thus they avoid re-reading the comments and therefore might not learn from the feedback. Alternatively, students may become so absorbed by the harsh comments that they stay stuck feeling dreadful about themselves and their abilities, again not learning from the feedback and therefore cannot improve. I really hope that examiners take on a different approach and utilise psychological theory in how they comment on each student's performance, praising where possible and nudging them to a better position through positive reinforcement.

- **Failing is not the end of the world.** Remember I mentioned earlier that there was the undertone of 3 strikes and you're out? Well, evidently it's not true but it is perhaps a hint of threat to drive learning, truly a fantastic reinforcement tool. If you do fail do not worry. You won't have to pack your stuff in boxes, the course will not kick you off. I think the only times when anyone would be kicked off the course is if they were found out to be behave in an unethical way and caused harm (or potential harm) to service users. If you fail, there will be processes that you follow which may include resitting your exam and discussing areas of concern with tutors. It will be ok. Please don't lose sleep over it.

Principle 32
Good quality learning far outweighs an excessive amount of poor knowledge.

Principle 33
Ensure that your basic human needs are met, otherwise nothing else matters nor will anything else be successful.

Principle 34
We all have good qualities and abilities, I am sure of it. It is devastating when this is neglected by others. But for your own sake, do not neglect yourself, your efforts, your positive qualities, and your abilities.

CHAPTER 19

Placements: Clinical work, political dramas, and feelings of hopelessness

"You cannot hope to build a better world without improving the individuals. To that end, each of us must work for our own improvement", Marie Curie.

Placement is a time for you to grow and develop clinically, to find out the type of clinician you want to be. At the start of each placement, you will often feel excited and apprehensive. You may be working in a field in which you are interested and keen to be, or it may be somewhere you know little about and / or dislike. We all have preferences regarding where we work and that's ok. Just be mindful of what your preferences are and allow yourself to be open to new experiences as well as the possibility that you may grow to love a certain area that you previously disliked.

It's the first day of a new placement. As you begin placement, there may be times when you feel nervous as you are overwhelmed by new everything – a new field of work, new team, new supervisor, new service users, and new techniques. Not only is everything new but the level of work expected of you is higher than what you may have been used to as an assistant. As time goes on and you begin to develop competency in this new area of work, you will also feel more and more confident in your abilities. And just like that, poof! Your placement draws to a close and you have to start the process all over again at your next placement.

- **Placement supervisor.** Your experience of each placement will depend on a multitude of factors, but perhaps the biggest factor affecting your placement is the relationship you have with your supervisor. I find that there are certain supervisors that you will always hold in mind throughout your career. You may hear their voice years after you have worked with them and this can influence your way of working. Your supervisors are placed in a position to be models for your therapeutic orientation, the approach you should take with the team and the service users, as well as the quality of your work. With this, the first supervisor you have during the course may be the one who has the biggest imprint on you. Their way of being can affect how you feel and think about future placements, what it is you believe supervisors will expect of you in terms of your work, and how safe it feels to ask for support (and how likely you will get it). As much as I would love to say that all supervisors are amazing, this would not be an accurate statement.

○ **You are in your infancy**: You have developed a lot of knowledge and skills throughout your time as an assistant psychologist; however things do level up on the clinical doctorate training. In a way, you are in your infancy of your qualified professional life. Mirroring developmental models, children rely on their primary caregivers for general growth, learning opportunities, and support. For healthy development to occur, children need to identify a 'safe base' so that they can develop a secure attachment with their caregiver. This allows them to feel safe enough to explore the outside world, knowing that their caregiver will be there to enjoy their development as well as supporting them when they need help. The key to secure attachment is the consistency of the caregiver's availability to support growth and meet the child's needs. Like this, we too need to develop a secure attachment to our supervisors. We want them to be consistently available for us, we feel safe enough to work that we can move away to work autonomously but also know that we can depend on them when we feel anxious and require support. We want them to be aware of our zone of proximal development: what we know and what we don't so they can build a scaffold to help us develop further. For this to occur in a healthy and safe way, we need our supervisors to be consistently available for us. Unfortunately, like some primary caregivers, the individuals who we look up to for developmental support may not have the capacity to support us in the way that we need. This may lead to what resembles ambivalent or avoidant attachment styles, where we feel anxious and uncomfortable around our supervisor and we may struggle to trust them for support. I have had supervisors on both sides of the spectrum – those who I have felt secure and safe with, as well as supervisors who I frankly disliked and I know this is true for other trainees. Sometimes we are unable to change our relationship with our supervisor – like with other people we come across in life, there are certain people who we will get on well with and others who we don't. As discussed later in this section, developing a supervisory contract and identifying a 'safe' clinical tutor from the university may allow you to create a reasonably healthy relationship with your supervisor wherein you can grow and develop appropriate skills from your placement.

o **Supervisor's own mental health**: Talking about this might surprise you, and it almost feels a little 'taboo' to mention it in this book but I believe it is a very real thing and thus should be noted. Any human being on this planet has 'mental health', as do you and your supervisor. Tragic things can happen to any of us at any time in life. For some trainees, you may be allocated a supervisor who is struggling with their mental wellbeing. Generally speaking, most supervisors will be aware of this and may inform the university course that they are unavailable to supervise trainees and thus trainees will not be in such circumstances. However, there are times this comes up unexpectedly with a trainee in place and this can be challenging on various levels. First, if the placement supervisor is still working, they may be unable to supervise you adequately or appropriately. Their capacity to think about your developmental needs, case load, and other relevant assignments may be limited and thus it can impact how supported you feel or how much you have learnt throughout your placement. The second way in which this can be challenging is that your supervisor may become completely absent; they may be off on long-term sickness leave and thus you are left alone. Either way, inadvertently it may feel they are inconsistently available which leaves you in a place of uncertainty; perhaps like a child you cling on for dear life to anyone qualified to support you or you detach and distance yourself for self-preservation. You almost have to fend for yourself and feed yourself with whatever knowledge and skills you have access to. Again, it is hoped that you can utilise your supervisory contract and support from your university clinical tutor to develop a sense of safety and ensure your clinical development.

o **Supervisor's relationship style:** Touching on the point around attachment styles, your supervisor will have their own attachment style with others based on their experiences. For instance, they may be leaning towards the ambivalent or avoidant attachment style, in which case this can impact how they are with you. This may not even be an obvious thing at first, but it may come out within subtleties of how they communicate with you. Alongside this, they may have particular internalised relationship patterns (or reciprocal roles) and such templates transpire in other relationships – including the one they have with you. They may have experienced criticism and high expectations in their line of work or personal life, and this may seep its way into how they speak to you; they may communicate criticism towards you and expect perfectionism from you. You may even witness them doing this with service users or other staff members. Scarily, not all qualified clinical psychologists are nice and wonderful and kind. Sadly not all are nice; some have an arrogant and punitive aura that surrounds them. Yes my bubble burst too when I witnessed this. One of my supervisors was unfortunately one of the least empathic people I have met and should not have worked in a place of care. This person was extremely critical without justification – not only to me but to our patients as well which was really upsetting. Perhaps this supervisor would have been better placed working in the military where you have to be cut off from human emotions and you're expected to shoot people. I was counting down the days till I said goodbye to you, you horrible person. I know I wasn't the only person to experience such an unkind and difficult supervisor; unfortunately, vile creatures roam among us. Hopefully, these people are the minority but still require extermination. If you do experience such difficulties I urge you to speak with your clinical tutor at the university to identify a solution to such a situation – the university should be in support of you. I have known people whereby such circumstances have been so difficult that they have been able to change placements thus changing supervisors. This was incredibly helpful, allowing them to feel safe with their supervisor and learn more from placement.

o **Your own relationship style**: Similarly, you too may have subtle ways of relating to others. From personal experience, a common characteristic I see in all psychologists is that we have high expectations of ourselves. This may be influenced by external factors, for example to get onto the clinical doctorate training, you have to work immensely hard. You may have had personal experiences whereby you feel others have been critical of you and you have had to behave in a particular way to be accepted by others. Such life experiences can influence how you are with others and it may mean that you become hypervigilant to certain interactions or signs. For example, if you have historically been criticised, you may become more sensitive to times of perceived criticism. This may then have an impact on your relationship with your supervisor. If they are expecting of you then you feel expected of, you may feel criticised that you are not working hard enough, which again can be an incredibly difficult experience.

o **Supervisory contract**: Upon starting a placement, you will have to complete a contract with your supervisor. This sometimes feels like a 'tick box' exercise but I would highly recommend that you take it seriously and spend some time thinking about what you would like from your supervisor and what you find unhelpful. Within this, think about the best teachers, mentors or supervisors you have ever had throughout your educational journey as well as career. What was it about your relationship with your supervisor that made it great? What was it that your supervisor did that helped you learn and develop? How can this be implemented in this new placement? You may also wish to think about any particular characteristics or interactions that you find difficult. This may be based on previous tutors or supervisory relationships you have had, or it may reflect more personal experiences. For instance, if you have personally struggled with the sense of feeling as though you are not good enough, you may consider criticism being difficult to hear, particularly if there is no helpful guidance attached to such comments. It may be that you feel out of your depth in this new line of work and so you wish to have direction. Alternatively, it might be that you have worked for years in such a field that you feel competent to retain a lot of autonomy and being micro-managed may feel restrictive or patronising. Whichever it is, consider everything that is helpful and unhelpful in a supervisor. Be open about this as it is your supervisor's duty to adapt their supervision style to be most helpful for you. More importantly, think about what you would do in the worst case scenario. For example, if you felt that you were not learning relevant skills, if you felt your supervisor was neglectful, if you felt unsafe in the workplace, or if you felt unable to speak to your supervisor freely. Be open with your future supervisor about what you would do in such circumstances, and document this in your supervisory contract. They too may have certain thoughts around what they would do in such situations if they felt a trainee was not meeting expectations or was practicing in an unsafe way. It is important for both of you to have an open discussion at the early stages of starting the placement so that expectations of both of you are known, and action plans to manage difficulties are clear. This is to protect both trainee and supervisor.

- **Workload**:
  - ○ **Caseload.** Typically, each placement has a general requirement that you see 6-8 service users, though the number may depend on the level of clinical complexity. Often this feels like a manageable number given the amount of time spent at placement. Your supervisor may be expecting you to see all of these service users from the start and some may stagger the times you begin work with patients to help your development. My first placement supervisor was incredible, he was so thoughtful of my needs and really supported my development. I started work with my caseload in a staggered way and supervision would involve reviews of how my caseload felt; if it was too much or too little, if there was sufficient variety for my development, and if there were similar presenting problems to consolidate my learning. He helped me work out when I could see them so it felt I had enough time to prepare before each session as well as reflect upon the sessions afterwards. He also attended the first session I had with each of the service users to help me work out first impressions of the work, how manageable it felt, how it would affect my development, and how I felt about seeing the individual for the duration of placement. This approach was extremely helpful and allowed me to have a great start to the clinical training course. He very much supported my needs and development. His approach was exceptional. I hope he reads this book as I still hold him in high regard and I hope to embody his methods with people I supervise.

In the early stages of meeting your placement supervisor, I would highly recommend suggesting such an approach as to how you may wish to begin placement. I appreciate not everyone would feel they need the same approach, for example perhaps not everyone wants to stagger their caseload and wish instead to jump in the deep end. Whichever approach you feel is more suited to your learning, I would suggest you recommend this where possible. I also suggest you keep an open dialogue around how your caseload feels throughout placement. I have known some trainees to end up with 10+ service users on their caseload which has felt overwhelming, while others feel that such a number is manageable given some of the work may be brief or short-lived. Similarly, some trainees have worked with 4 or 5 service users on their caseload and although this may sound too little, it has stretched the person's learning as the service users have many complex needs and are at high risk. For such trainees, placement time may also be occupied with other pieces of work including joint work with a member of the multidisciplinary team, family work, facilitating group therapy, training staff, and auditing or completing service related research. Such variety in work may impact the number of people you have on your caseload. Along with this, have conversations with your supervisor around mandatory pieces of work you are required to complete (e.g. a case utilising CBT) as well as types of work you are interested in so that you are able to enhance your skills in these areas. Reviewing your caseload and the type of work you are doing on a frequent basis can make the difference between an excellent placement and a mediocre one.

○ **Facilitating staff training.** This was certainly a helpful experience and I would advise that if possible, you seek an opportunity to facilitate staff training throughout your placement. This can help your development in a multitude of ways: strengthen your learning about a certain topic; overcome anxieties around public speaking; enhance and adapt your communication style; identify ways to engage others and support their learning; manage a group situation; and ensure organisational skills. These are all skills that are going to be required of you as a qualified clinical psychologist so try to find ways of building these skills while you can and you are protected under the title of trainee. The training I facilitated for staff was on CBT for psychosis which was supported by my supervisor. It was useful in that I had the opportunity to develop some of the skills mentioned above but more importantly I look back now and I can identify things that I could have improved on and I would do differently today. It has shaped how I engage staff in training sessions, particularly as some staff sign up to training as a day out of the office with little intention to learn. It has made me a lot more creative in the way I hold sessions so that even if staff do not wish to learn or are a little resistant to psychological models, they go away with a different feeling and different experience, opening their mind to the subject and increasing their motivation to learn more.

o **Audits and service related projects.** As a part of the training programme, some of the universities will require you to complete an audit at one of your placements and / or a service related project in another. This can either go well and be an easy experience or it can be incredibly infuriating and feel meaningless. To avoid hating life for the duration of this project, I advise you to keep in mind the following to make your life easier and ensure the project feels useful, rather than a paperwork exercise. Be sure you understand the exact process of either project before setting it up. Many people I trained with (and surprisingly some supervisors), struggled to identify the differences between audits and service related projects. The differences may seem subtle on the surface but they are distinct.

In summary, audits must follow an exact procedure to examine an ideal standard of practice which is set up by the service/NHS/guidelines against what is actually happening; explore the difference; and make recommendations to reduce the difference so that actual practice can become more in line with the standard practice. This means that the question set up must be very specific to the audit standards and the steps you would take to examine the question should be clear and logical. One of my audit questions related to service waiting times: the standard for waiting time was X number of weeks to access the service; are we meeting this? I then looked at the referral list over the past 6 months and calculated the waiting times, documenting the proportion of people who were seen within the 'national expected' waiting time as well as those who had to wait longer. I explored reasons around the longer wait time and discussed recommendations around reducing waiting times. I advised when this standard should be reviewed again to ensure recommendations were put in place and whether these recommendations were useful or if alternative measures were required. When you understand the process, it becomes an easy project. Don't over complicate it and be very clear about your process. Service related projects may relate to a particular need within the service. Your project therefore aims to explore what is available to meet this need and provide recommendations for the service as well as service providers (i.e. the people who fund the service). These recommendations are hoped to result in patients having their needs met.

Please understand this clear distinction between the two projects, as people who do not often risk failing the project and have to complete it in another placement – weeks of wasted effort for nothing. There is plenty of information online around how to complete an audit and service related project. Use this as guidance. Finally, I recommend that you do a project that is of interest to you and that is actually meaningful for the service. I find it infuriating engaging in work that is meaningless as it is boils down to a lot of effort with little use or implication. What is the point? Given you have to do the project anyway, be sure it is something that can be of help to someone.

- **Multi-disciplinary teamwork.** Like many things on this course, this can be great or this can be horrendous. I sincerely hope you enjoy this work but either way, it will be an experience and will help you learn a lot about the benefits and difficulties of working within a multi-disciplinary team (or frankly with other people in general). As we know, working with other people is fantastic as it can open our eyes to new ways of thinking, enhance our learning, and confirm our decision making. We have a better chance of supporting service users in a holistic sense and we can share responsibility over care and risk in order to support service users. Unfortunately, this is not always the case so get ready for office drama and politics! For example, you will meet care coordinators who will seem to be permanently absent, but if you pop into a Topshop you will sure enough find them there. You might find other staff members who are hateful of psychology and look down upon you and your decisions (perhaps through jealousy that you are paid more / seen as higher skilled). 'Cliques' may transpire among certain members of the team where they create the sense that they are more 'popular' and therefore clever and know what they are talking about. Just to say, no you are not popular and nor are you that intelligent, you are only those things in your own mind. Receptionists should certainly not be making judgements on mental capacity and moreover, shame on qualified professionals who blindly take on such opinions to make clinical decisions. During your professional career, you may also identify people who are engaging in malpractice as noted by any of the professional registration bodies. This is obviously extremely concerning and in such circumstances, whistleblowing to either the Trust or relevant registration body is then required. You do not have to be a qualified member of staff to take these steps and it is encouraged that you voice your opinions and concerns as it is ultimately vital to patient care. Like they say, allowing malpractice to occur and not responding is almost as bad as engaging in dangerous practice yourself. If you ever do need support to take these steps I encourage you to speak to your tutors at the university for support.

Principle 35
Take your time finding your feet, the type of clinician you wish to become, and the style you wish to embrace.

Principle 36
Never forget the importance of your relationship with your supervisor. You can only be nurtured from a healthy relationship, and to that end, lay a foundation from which you can have a safe and secure relationship.

Principle 37
Work within your zone of competency. Be mindful of your workload and notice what is manageable, what would help you grow, and what would stunt your growth. Remember, growth may be uncomfortable at times but involving benefits to your own development is essential.

Principle 38
Never shy away from voicing your concerns.

CHAPTER 20
Research thesis

"You'll be damned if you do, and damned if you don't", Eleanor Roosevelt.

Oh, did they not tell you? This may make you want to rip your hair out of your scalp or squeeze lemon juice into your eyes. Too much? Hmm you might feel differently when you start this project. Hopefully, many of you will have a great experience completing this piece of work. Don't worry if not, I'm going to try my best to guide you through it and I hope that the knowledge of 'this is indeed sh*t' will be validating for the struggles you're going through. Also please don't forget the fact that this research project and everything that comes with it must come to an end. Let's begin.

- **Initial stages.** I don't know what they do on your course, but for many, academic tutors and researchers throughout the university will plan an open day to speak to trainees about their field of interest and potential research ideas. These tutors already have a research question in mind, something they have been wanting to complete but perhaps have not had the time to do and / or are too tired to do as they have been awake for the past 15 years straight doing other pieces of research to obtain their title of Senior Lecturer, Senior Reader (no it's not just you, I didn't realise this was a real title either), or Professor. When this day comes, I recommend you do the following.

  o **Have an open mind**. Even when a particular project title or research area is not at all what you would expect yourself to be drawn to. What you will often find is that 'sexier' subjects such as psychosis are often snapped up quickly so there will be many other people who will want to work with this tutor / do this project. This reduces the likelihood that you will get your project of choice. Also, given these projects are more in demand, the research question often becomes a lot more complicated and more effort and work is required of you. During the initial stage you may think that the research question is doable and interesting but give it a few months and you will discover how much more challenging it is than what first meets the eye. So, please keep your mind open even if it is just by a few centimetres. Those of you targeting a particular research area with tunnel vision will be in pain later. I can hear you say, "I'd much rather do something I am interested in even if it's hard work and, it will be hard work anyway so". Ah, you think you're smart, well done Margaret. Well, you may end up with your attractive topic of choice, but at least keep an open mind to begin with.

- o **Choosing your supervisor**. Take your time thinking about the qualities of each of your potential research supervisors. As much as they may be introducing the topic area to you and they may seem to have all the knowledge and expertise, really think about the qualities of the person you would like to be supervising you. Let's even start with the basics, such as wanting this person to be nice and kind? How does that sound? No, I'm not trying to be patronising. Believe me, you are going to be desperate for someone who is kind and thoughtful as this course progresses, life throws garbage at you, and you still have this massive piece of research to do. Generally speaking, any of the tutors are essentially going to be competent enough in their area of research as they have gotten to that stage in their career. You want them to be supportive, to be responsive to your needs, and to match up with your personality and relationship style. As much as you are doing this research with them and they want you to be competent to do this research, you need them to be competent enough to be your supporter and supervisor.

- o **Planning stages.** This is fun. Plan your research questions and off you pop. In reality your research plans change and they will change a number of times as you start to really think about it and work out how you are going to go about it. You will come across obstacles and thus need to find ways of overcoming these hurdles, which results in your research question and processes changing. You will probably plan and re-plan all the way throughout the research until the day you submit your thesis. Filled with a sense of security? I know, uncertainty often evokes a sense of anxiety as we feel unsafe and insecure, not knowing the future. However, the more we are able to tolerate and accept a level of uncertainty, the more secure we feel and indeed the easier the research process will feel as we are not holding onto certain ideas. Here, you may wish to practice non-attachment and I would say this is perhaps the best thing I have ever done. My initial project idea was around examining the effectiveness of a specific type of therapy in primary care services; however, this very quickly changed to how people with dementia perceived helpful communication. Not only did the question change but so did the entire research area. These things happen and in all fairness, I'm glad it changed as the initial project idea would have been infeasible and too taxing (I think I would have aged 58 years), while the research I actually did was manageable and I ended up finding it interesting despite never envisaging myself working with older adults. The main thing is working out what research question is feasible to do. Throughout the course, you will be juggling 103 ceramic plates and so figuring out what you could do without dropping more than 50 of those plates is crucial. Aiming for something very complex and / or that requires a lot of time and energy may mean that you will fall short and you will have a mental breakdown. It is better do a piece of good quality research even if it appears straightforward, compared to a very interesting and complicated piece of research to a poor standard.

o **Application to research ethics.** This can feel like such a drag. It goes on for ages, the forms are unbelievably long, and you have to repeat yourself a few times. As painful as this process may seem it can be a helpful exercise in that this will really help you plan out your research questions and the specifics of how you will carry out this research. If you see this as a paper exercise, you will hate life. If you see it as an aide to helping you plan your research project, identify pitfalls as well as ways to overcome such barriers, this will be of great help. Consider why is this research question important, how and why is it useful to stakeholders, and how you could realistically complete this research project given the time frame you have.

- **Doing the thing.** I love research. It might have sounded like I don't but I think research is important. It is essentially what helps humanity grow and develop. What I don't like is the rubbish you get around it that makes the whole thing a lot harder. Having a good supervisor and a feasible project make a huge difference to how painful the process is, but there will be other hurdles to overcome which too can be exhausting.

  o **Recruitment.** Generally speaking, you will be recruiting a clinical sample, i.e. people who use a clinical service. To gain as many participants as possible, you are going to have to advertise like you've never advertised before (and if you're British, you are likely to feel shy about this). Chances are you will have to go into professional teams and speak to clinicians about your project and ask them to tell their patients about you and your project, recommending they sign up. You may very well feel like you are begging and this is perhaps the worst thing. No one likes someone who is desperate. Embrace the attitude that you are giving the clinician and the service user the opportunity to express themselves, feel heard, and have an impact on future care. I have previously come across clinicians who describe seeking service users as 'unethical' but how unethical is it to deny the individual of this opportunity to take part? I am being serious when I say you are not an inconvenience to professionals and they have the privilege to be offered this opportunity for them and their patients. It's just a shame that some people feel so overwhelmed in their work that it narrows the space in their brain to consider research projects. Either that or they're a bit stupid. Chin up, you'll be awesome.

- **Participants**. I love interacting with participants, this is the best part of the entire research project. You actually speak to normal humans unlike the people you've been interacting with at the university and you get to talk to them about anything and everything. Like anything relating to our line of profession, sometimes you will come across participants who are really struggling emotionally and / or mentally and will require extra support. That's where your clinical skills come in. You may have to liaise with their care coordinator or responsible clinician to ensure their safety and that they receive the support required. This can add time to your workload but it is a process that obviously cannot be missed. Furthermore, recording aspects around such incidents and reflecting upon it in your thesis can work in your favour as you are demonstrating a direct link between the research question and the clinical effects and needs. Devastatingly, there are rare occasions whereby a participant might die, which could be caused by different reasons. I really hope this does not happen but if you or your colleague experience such a tragic event, I sincerely hope that you are able to get support from your supervisors and tutors around this. Take a break from the research project and review ethical guidelines. Get support external to the course or your tutors. It's ok to feel sad, just do whatever it is you need to do. Do not feel pressured by course tutors / research supervisors. We are all human (even though some of the researchers feel more like robots). We all need time to process and heal. Research is a people industry, not an emotionless one.

- **Oops.** Mistakes can be made very easily throughout the research process and write up. These mistakes are especially easy to make if your supervisor trusts you have done the right thing without checking or does not really know what should be done. For example, I made a massive error in my systematic review. In its early stages, I selected a few search terms which I believed were appropriate; however, the way in which I conducted my search was incorrect. Unfortunately, I only discovered this after I had submitted it to a peer reviewed journal whereby one of the reviewers pointed this out to me. You can only imagine my pain. Luckily, I had completed this paper quite early on during the clinical training course so I had time to amend it. However, because the error was so early on in the procedure of the study I had to essentially redo the entire search, analysis, and write up. Egh. Please do not make the same mistake I did. I confidently thought I was doing the right thing without really giving it much thought and without checking it with other people who were more expert in such studies. I had never completed a systematic review before and in hindsight I don't really think I knew what I was doing. That was my fault and I was irresponsible. Please take on responsibility for your study wholly. No one else is going to save you if you don't do it yourself. Your supervisors may miss such errors as well and will not necessarily take care over this project as you would. Even if you think you are engaging in the correct process, check and double check it with others who are more skilled and expert than you. This may feel like it takes a bit more time to begin with but it will save you time in the long-term as you will have completed the study properly and appropriately.

o **Analysis.** Follow the appropriate analysis tools and protocol for answering your research question. You may need to temporarily pretend that you're a robot and make sure that you follow such processes step by step in a logical way. Even when you're doing a qualitative analysis and this requires self-reflection and introspection, do it in a way that is logical and procedural. In this way, your analysis should lead to relevant conclusions.

Sometimes we do not always get the results we wanted or expected to see. That's ok and it happens to most of us. Consider this, most of the research that is published out there is accepted for publication because it demonstrates something interesting (as well as the study being well thought out). That suggests that there is a bunch of other studies that have been completed that might not show anything too significant. Don't be tempted to sneakily skew your results to indicate that you have discovered something earth shattering that no one has ever considered before. Skewing or massaging the results to show something more interesting than what they actually say will not help. You will be found out and you will just have to redo the process again. This is also true for people who do not follow the precise procedure required for answering the research question. Again, try to detach yourself from your human being, pretend you are Spock from Star Trek, and identify the appropriate procedure because "it's only logical". I had to look this up because I don't actually know the difference between Star Trek and Star Wars (please don't throw eggs at me), but this quote is useful in helping us consider the mindset you need to take to pass this thesis. If possible, check your analysis process with someone else who is an expert in the field. Even if you don't know anyone who is an expert in the field, check your analysis with someone else who can read and follow instructions. Give them the instructions for the analysis methodology as dictated by the grace of Google (or Andy Field for stats) and ask them to follow the process. See if they come to the same or similar results as you. Doing this with someone who has no emotional or mental investment in your research is helpful as they are more likely to follow the analysis process correctly and get you to the place you need to be.

o   **Write up.** Keep it simple, stupid. You don't have to use fancy language or make this look extra complicated. You are essentially aiming for your papers to be understood by an average 7 year old. If you can explain a complex idea to a child, then you have truly understood what you are doing, what the project aims and shows, and your readers will be grateful. Explain everything you have completed in logical and simple steps so anyone can follow your train of thought and come to the same understanding and conclusions. When we are particularly stressed and working on something that is complicated, we then begin to use complex language and we begin to get confused ourselves. I don't know about you, but I become irritated by looking at research papers that involve complex (and incomprehensible) language, that I have to look up every other word. Some researchers purposefully use complex language for 2 main reasons. First, they like to have their ego stroked and make it appear that they are a genius, they should be respected to the upmost, and they are higher than other people. Second, by using such language they can cover up the fact that their study was average and scare people off from attempting to do a better job of it. For such researchers I say, what the heck? You wouldn't even be around to hear a potential reader say, "wow this researcher must be clever" so you wouldn't be getting that ego boost anyway. Plus your very actions are the thing that is hindering research from progressing society further and faster than what could have been. Sadly, all your paper does is make it hard to decipher the real meaning of the study. For us readers and normal people just trying to get through life and this training course, we cannot control what other people do, we can only control what we do. Let me say that again, we cannot control others, we can only control ourselves, our actions, and our choices. Do yourself a favour and make your papers easy to understand. This will be of substantial benefit to your examiners as the easier your paper is to understand and logical steps are apparent throughout, the less questioning you will face from them and the less errors or comments you will have to respond to. In addition, taking this approach will be helpful for you if and when you decide to submit your paper for publication. Future readers will benefit from it, you are more likely to be referenced, and information is more easily disseminated so thus it can have a more meaningful impact.

- **Examination around your thesis aka 'Viva'.** The 'viva' is a spoken exam you will face about your thesis, wherein experts in the field will ask you about your research. People prepare like crazy for this day, like it is the day that will determine everything. In all fairness, yes it is important, but so are all the other days you've lived through on the course as well as days outside of the course. This is not the 'life determiner'; your life is bigger and better than this. Keep in mind that this day is not much more significant than all those other submission dates you did for your assignments, exams, or placement reviews. Stay strong! You can do this and it will pass. You may have been allocated an examiner who seems quite scary usually or you may have been allocated someone who seems nice. Strangely, those examiners who are usually frightening change persona and are actually really friendly during this process. They may even help you to come up with the answer they are looking for. People spend a long time panicking about their viva, preparing and practicing. In reality there is actually little that can be done to prepare for this day. It is what it will be. There will be things that come up which you may have anticipated as well as questions that you would have never dreamed of being asked. It's incredibly hard to predict. What I will say is that your viva often just feels like a chat about your studies, that's all. It's really not that bad or frightening.

In the morning of your viva, get exercising, practice some deep breathing through mindfulness, and get your zen on. Then you are ready to go. Trust in yourself. It can be nerve-wracking but just remember, the examiners are human too and they're no better than you or I. Everyone wipes their arse the same way.

Principle 39

"Whether you think you can or you think you can't, you're right", Henry Ford.

Principle 40

Keep an open mind and allow the direction of your research to be dictated by what is feasible, manageable, meaningful, and useful.

Principle 41

Other researchers are simply human beings like you or me. Do not get absorbed into the hierarchical power dynamics.

CHAPTER 21
Your wellbeing is the most important thing

"Everything can be taken from a man, but the last of the human freedoms: to choose one's attitudes in any given set of circumstances", Victor Frankl.

Most of you are unlikely to have received the message that your wellbeing is of upmost importance from any of your tutors or supervisors. This is extremely sad and heart-breaking because this is the most important message of all. All of my terrible jokes aside, if you take anything away from this book, it should be this: you are important, your wellbeing is important, and your mental health is important. If you are not well and your physical and psychological wellbeing is not prioritised, then nothing else matters. What is the point of becoming 'successful' if you are not ok to actually enjoy it and live it? It doesn't make sense. This entire journey can be soul destroying. It can break you again and again. It is very testing and it is perhaps designed in such a way as demand and desire to be a psychologist is so high that the elders needed to come up with a way of determining who is 'deserving'. Some people become willing to sacrifice everything in order to get there. Let me tell you though, it is not worth your life, your wellbeing or your happiness. Life should be about so much more and is so much bigger than this job title. It is ludicrous that some people believe that it is ok to sacrifice their physical health and sanity in order to 'please the course'. You are a human being and you have basic needs that need to be met. You deserve to be healthy and happy. You do not need to be miserable. You do not need to feel on edge all the time and that you are subpar or that you are not good enough. Please consider that this career, whichever stage you are in – whether that be as an assistant or trainee – it is a job at the end of the day. Nothing more and nothing less. You are being paid for your time there and that is all. You can go in, complete the tasks you need to do in the hours you have, and get out. You are not required to be thinking about it day and night. Like anyone else, you too have other things going on in life such as your friends, family, relationships, events, physical health, a home etc. These things also matter. The course does not deserve you sacrificing other things in life. Regain control and establish equilibrium. Prioritise yourself, your health, and your wellbeing.

Relationships

"We need four hugs a day for survival. We need 8 hugs a day for maintenance. We need 12 hugs a day for growth", Virginia Satir.

We are social creatures. We depend on others for survival and for our emotional wellness. Without relationships, we can struggle. We may rely on others for support and they can provide us with something that we find hard to provide ourselves. When we are down in the dumps and beating ourselves up, they can give us love, care, and compassion. They may sometimes know us better than we know ourselves and give us what we need when we need it the most. Other people can give meaning to our lives. They might be the answer to our personal why and what drives us, what motivates us, what gives us joy, and what makes us smile. Of course different relationships feel different; we may know people to different extents, feel safe and close to certain people while we may distance ourselves from others. We may allow ourselves to be vulnerable with specific individuals, exposing our true experiences, thoughts and feelings, particularly when we feel secure and stable. The less secure and more unsafe we feel, the less likely we are willing to share our true selves with that person. This goes for all types of relationships, family, friends, and romantic partners. Working as an assistant psychologist or being a trainee clinical psychologist can be incredibly difficult, it challenges you and stretches you with respect to your knowledge, your personality, and your emotional wellness. There will be plenty of times when you will experience distress that has been evoked by supervisors, tutors, examiners, and other external sources. Tragically, this can have a massive negative impact on our personal lives. As much as being an assistant or trainee is technically a 'job', sometimes that comes home with you and you can't help it because it is so overwhelming. You may find yourself struggling with certain relationships in your personal life: you may begin to withdraw from others, arguments with people who you are close to become more frequent, other relationships become more unboundaried and uncontained, and you may find yourself resenting certain people. Certain relationships become strained and following ruptures, some feel near enough impossible to heal.

I've witnessed many people breaking up with their partners during this period. This is upsetting as the initial features leading up to the breakup were stressful and breakups in themselves are stressful, making life harder. What is extremely sad is that this feels almost instigated by the line of this profession and the approach people take to it. For example, the training doctorate course will push you outside of any zone in which you feel comfortable, it will degrade you and you will feel about 1 inch tall. This in itself reduces how safe you feel in general; you are continuously on edge, anxiously awaiting the next attack and finding ways to defend yourself. You are essentially living in threat mode. This sense cannot be turned off like a switch as soon as you leave the building and go home, so unfortunately when you go home you may also feel like you are in threat mode. Things that were easy to do are suddenly a lot harder and feel more effortful. It feels like other people who do not engage in this career do not really understand how stressful it is, how much pressure you are under, and how this process is breaking you. Your capacity to show love, affection, and care may also be negatively impacted as your energy resources are depleted. You cannot pour out of an empty jug, and this course definitely drains your jug. You may become more sensitive to seemingly small comments and incidents which somehow blow up to astronomical levels. The more unsafe you feel, the less of your true self you are willing to show. You conceal from others, particularly those who do not understand, as this feels like a risky process. You conceal to protect your vulnerability and avoid destruction. This may mean that relationships feel more detached and distant. They may feel less meaningful or pleasurable. Everything just feels a lot harder. This in turn has an impact on how you perform throughout your course as your energy to focus on the work is reduced. A horrible catch 22 cycle.

The only way I managed this is by trying to be fixed with certain 'appointments' I had with friends or my significant other at the time. For example, I would make sure that from Friday evening till Sunday evening I had something planned that was concrete and I would feel bad about cancelling. I would plan to see my friends and / or partner, go out for dinner, go for a day trip, binge watch a TV series, and go out of town. I would make sure that I was spending every bit of time either outside of my house and / or with other people. This meant that I was forced to get out of the area which was associated with doing work and I was suddenly surrounded by something very different. Even if I was stressed and reluctant to go out, I couldn't help but enjoy myself as I got to do things I liked with people I loved. I knew I would feel bad about cancelling because I had already committed to someone - use that positive 'guilt' feeling to your advantage. There were other times when I planned to do something on my own because I either had too much stimulation from other people and wanted a bit of me time or because other people were too busy. I know a lot of people may say in their mind that is what they would like to do and they enjoy their own company, but unfortunately they very easily slip into doing work because the guilt from not doing work gnaws away at them. And hey, given they have the free time now, why not. But no, I would say this is not the right approach. You need to commit to yourself that you are going to give yourself the day. You are deserving of the day to enjoy as you wish, and if you end up doing work, then you are breaking that commitment to yourself and you are denying yourself that thing you deserve. Why would you deny yourself this? If you don't give yourself this time and energy, it is you who suffers and you are neglected. Be kind to yourself and give yourself what you deserve.

Throughout this career path, some relationships will end. This is not necessarily your fault or the fault of the career. Sometimes relationships just simply need to end and you feel this when you recognise that your relationships with certain people are not in alignment with you, your values, or what you want. Over the years of working towards qualifying as a clinical psychologist, you will change as a person. You will not be the same individual you were when starting the journey and nor should you be. You will learn, develop, and grow. With this, you will learn a lot about yourself as well as other people. You will remember people who helped you when things got hard, people who left you when things got hard, and people who made things harder for you. You will start developing strength in your own personhood – either because you were encouraged by positive influencers and motivators or because you were pushed down and beaten up which left you no choice but to be resilient. You may feel secure in yourself and your abilities as you have been shown compassion and assurance or you might continue to feel insecure due to the years of uncertainty instilled in you. Whichever way it goes, please recognise what has led you to this place and the people who have supported you throughout. Consider who replenished and refuelled your energy sources and who drained these. Keep hold of relationships which nourished you and prioritise these throughout your career journey as these will be the people who will help carry you through life. This is far more important than what this career path would ever give you. These people will also help you succeed through this career journey as they can provide you with the sense of safety and security, from which is the best place to learn, work, and develop. If you recognise that some relationships simply do not help you but continuously take away from you, it is ok for these to end or for you to at least limit your contact with such people. You are worthy of receiving compassion, care, and security from others and so if you do not get this from someone, you do not need to invest your time and energy in them. As painful as it is, letting go of some people can be one of the best things that you do. It can give you space for better people to walk in and stay.

Psychological wellbeing

"The face is that when you make the other suffer, he will try to find relief by making you suffer more. The result is an escalation of suffering on both sides", Thich Nhat Hanh.

For me, I feel like trainee's personal psychological wellbeing on the clinical doctorate course is the very definition of irony. Working and training to become a clinical psychologist and our own personal psychological wellbeing is neglected. Bravo! We don't need to pay attention to our own psychological wellbeing surely, because if we read books and study hard enough it all solves itself, right? Egh, wrong. You can't 'psychologise' yourself. Believe me I've tried many times. It feels stupid as [expletives]. You can look at yourself from a theoretical standpoint, sure, but that way it's almost like reading a book or working on a case rather than being connected to yourself in an emotional and mental way. You become detached and as much as you might 'know' it, you only know it logically, not emotionally. Your head and your heart are in completely different places. They cannot be united because you yourself become the blockage. There are certain unconscious processes and defence mechanisms occurring in the background that you cannot control thus cannot 'work on yourself'. In summary, you need someone else to help you think about what's going on for you and reach a better place.

As time has passed, I believe the clinical training courses have become much more aware of trainees' psychological wellbeing though I am unsure how much is being done to support this as such. I know certain clinical tutors and supervisors who are absolutely amazing and are so supportive, so mindful of the individual's wellbeing and who are able to meet the person's needs. I wish we had more people like this. Unfortunately, personal psychological wellbeing may not be top of the agenda. This may be due to a multitude of factors:

- Tutors and supervisors have different goals to assistant psychologists or trainees and are therefore blind to their needs and psychological wellbeing.

- Tutors and supervisors come from a critical place and are too inside their mind to consider an alternative, compassionate and empathic approach.

- Tutors and supervisors are ultimately focused on work outcome rather than anything related to the person themselves. FYI – this is the main reason for low productivity and high turnover of staff in many employment sectors as employees feel uncared for, dismissed, and rejected.

- This career path gears you up for self-sacrifice. You have to work extremely hard to very high standards to succeed due to its competitiveness. This means you are constantly working hard to serve and please others, inadvertently neglecting yourself in the process. You would have little time for yourself and thus your psychological wellbeing deteriorates in the process.

Whatever it is that has affected you, please do not neglect your own psychological wellbeing. If you are not ok emotionally and psychologically, nothing else matters. Your wellbeing should be the top of your priority, and it is a priority. You deserve to be well and you can only develop and progress in life, your career, finances, friendships, and relationships if you are feeling well emotionally and psychologically. We are in the business of care and how ironic is it that we are the last people to expect to receive that care. We care for other people, whether that be service users or people in our personal lives, because we have an obvious role to do so. We have external relationships with these people that involve contact and compassion with them, and so this encompasses the care we provide for them. But remember, as much as we have relationships with other people, we also have a relationship with ourselves. If we provide care for ourselves, we too are the person who is receiving that care. If we do not provide care for ourselves, we are the person who is neglected. Like a parent-child relationship, we need to nurture that inner child within us and be wise enough to recognise what is helpful for our wellbeing.

Self-care

"You can search throughout the entire universe for someone who is more deserving of your love and affection than you are yourself, and that person is not to be found anywhere. You, yourself, as much as anybody in the entire universe, deserve your love and affection", author Unknown.

You will hear many supervisors and tutors in clinical settings as well as the training course who will talk about and advise 'self-care'. It is vital that we receive care, whether that be from ourselves or from others, as we need that care to survive and be our optimal selves. I completely believe that it is possible and important for us to self-care as well. However, I do sometimes question what is self-care? It feels like a term that's been overused but it is rare for people to speak about what it actually looks like or involves. The bottom line is it is anything that you feel fits for you at that time. Self-care can look different at different times and mean different things. It might involve caring for different aspects of ourselves which may involve immediate or delayed care. For example, I exercise on a regular basis and for me this is self-care. As much as I have days in which I don't feel like exercising, I still do it because I know that it makes me feel better in the long-term and if I don't exercise, I'm grouchy and miserable. Immediate self-care for me may be going to the shop and eating a pack of donuts in one go. Clearly, I'm an advocate of a balanced lifestyle as shown by example. Simply put, do whatever it is that you need to do, this might vary at different points in your life, and this might not always look 'healthy'. For example, self-care does not necessarily have to involve meditating at the top of a mountain for 10 hours, for some people it might be drinking a glass (or bottle) of wine. Spend some time thinking about what it is that is most helpful for you, why is this helpful, what need does it fulfil, and how do you feel doing it. Schedule in time to do whatever activity this is. Prioritise it. Our to do list, demands, and tasks may appear a lot and overwhelming but they do not take priority over our own needs. Make an appointment with yourself to do whatever it is you need to do and commit to this. As much as you give to other people (which you will do a lot in your career), it is equally important to give to yourself. If you don't give to yourself, it is also you who is being neglected in the process. If you give to yourself, you yourself gets nourished.

I cannot stress how important and necessary it is to self-care and to do this regularly; even when you feel you are feeling 'ok'. If anything, when you are feeling generally well, that's the best time to engage in self-care. This is for two primary reasons. First, your capacity to self-care is higher as you have more time and head-space to do this. Second, you will build up your 'resilience baseline' which means you would feel better overall, noticing an improvement in your wellbeing and reduction in your stress levels. Attempting to self-care only during times when you are struggling and it becomes urgent is near enough impossible – engaging in self-care is hardest when you need it the most. Prioritising your own needs and wellbeing on a regular day to day basis means that your life would generally feel better, your tolerance to difficult situations are higher, and you would feel more content. This is essential to surviving throughout your career journey as a student, assistant psychologist, and trainee clinical psychologist.

Personal therapy

"Our wounds are often the openings into the best and most beautiful parts of us", David Richo.

I find it fascinating that you are required to receive personal therapy as a part of other therapy training programmes. This goes for psychotherapy, counselling, cognitive analytical therapy etc. But not clinical psychology! No, we're better than that. Apparently. Who needs that level of self-reflection and support anyway? Fools I tell you! I wish you could see my facial expression as I am writing this as the concept that clinical psychologists do not need therapy is absurd. If anything, it becomes a frequent conversation that we have that "everyone could do with therapy", but why not us? One rule for us and another for everyone else, because psychologists have the magical power, knowledge, and insight?

I am a massive advocate for having personal therapy. Whoever you are and whatever stage of life you are in. I have had several bouts of therapy throughout life: as a teenager, in my early 20's, mid 20's, and early 30's. Each time I have had therapy it has been a completely different experience, and that is perhaps because I am a completely different person looking at my life through different lenses each time. I suspect it would be the same for you if you chose to go to therapy. Sometimes, bad things happen to us and we cannot have control over them, and when there are so many things that are happening, we can feel overwhelmed and swamped. This is particularly true when you are on the clinical doctorate course; you experience multiple co-occurring demands at placement, at university, and in your personal life. The more you are holding, the less space you have for coping well. Even if it feels like nothing too bad is going on, it can still be helpful to go to therapy to have that space. Often we only approach therapy when we are really struggling which is perhaps the time when we have less headspace to reflect and understand. This is also the time when we are in most distress and are less able to regulate our emotions. Attending therapy before things get too difficult may be a more helpful way to support ourselves and our own wellbeing, reducing the risk of falling into an abyss. Even if it feels like things are manageable, but perhaps on the edge, therapy may be a helpful way to gain further insight to reach a resolution.

"Practice what you preach" and not "do as I say and not as I do". Perhaps one of the best reasons to attend therapy, particularly during this career journey, is that it provides you with the real felt experience of what it is like to receive therapy. What experiences do service users have? What are the highs and the lows of being a service user? What is the most important thing when having therapy? That is perhaps why other therapy training courses require you to receive therapy to promote self-reflection of your own personal experiences and baggage, as well as your therapeutic practice. The most impactful therapy I have ever received was indeed the one I took during my clinical training doctorate. Of course this was not mandatory, but I sought it out. Initially I approached therapy because I was struggling in my personal life. Remember what I said earlier about relationships breaking down? Mine felt tragic at the time and psychologising myself was not cutting it. Going to therapy felt so impactful was for two main reasons: it gave me insight into myself as well as insight into being a service user. I am not going to go into how it influenced my personal life as it is not relevant for this book, but I will go into how it affected my perceptions of being a service user and clinician.

I remember the first appointment I had with the therapist. I was nervously waiting in the waiting room before she came out. I was shocked as to how anxious I was to begin this process. I had been to therapy before, I deliver therapy in my day job, so I thought to myself, "why am I so anxious? I'm familiar with how this goes". For some reason I could not shake off that anxiety. It was an awful feeling. I was perhaps so anxious because I knew I was going to expose myself and allow myself to be vulnerable to someone else, a complete stranger. I remember thinking to myself and praying under my breath in that waiting room that the therapist was nice. That's all I could think of and all I wanted at the time. I didn't even care if she was incompetent or unskilled in the therapy type; all

I wanted was for her to be nice to me. And honestly, I was not expecting myself to come out with something like that. Putting my hands up, I'm usually the type of person who has certain expectations of others, not necessarily expecting the best thing in the world, but I expect some level of competency and knowledge. This was totally different though. All of my usual expectations went out of the window and I wanted someone who would be kind to me and tell me that I am ok as a human being and I am worthy of existing. I may have been more like this because of how sensitive and distraught I was feeling in general but facing the reality of meeting a therapist made me really consider what actually mattered. My therapist was wonderful, it felt safe to continue seeing her again and I felt really sad when I knew that our relationship would come to an end. It was a difficult feeling which caused me to consider how much do I share with my therapist, it affected my expectations of therapy, and how much she could help me. This experience essentially made me think of what it would be like to be a patient, how would patients respond to endings of relationships, and how much would they feel safe to share as with sharing comes vulnerability. I still think about this therapist years after I have seen her and it's only been with time that I have been able to see how skilled and competent she really was. I suppose this really inspired me in terms of the therapist I want to be; that safe space for someone and to help positive change to continue long after therapy has ended. It also made me think of the limitations dictated by the NHS around how much care can be provided and how this can let down some service users.

Life is full of ups and downs which we cannot always have control over or manage well. Tragedies do happen and this occurs irrespective of your line of work or the stage of your career. Attending therapy is ok and there is no shame in it. It's so strange because I have known psychologists and therapists to shy away from attending therapy which makes me wonder whether they too hold a sense of stigma to the idea; even though they promote that therapy is acceptable and a safe space. You don't have to attend therapy yourself and no one is forcing you to, but I do highly recommend it even if it is brief. As much as we 'know' about therapy, logical knowledge and emotional experiences of its reality are two very different things. Only by doing therapy we can really understand what it is like, we can remove our inner demons, and really reduce and manage stigma. Through therapy, our head and heart are more likely to unite and we can move further towards our values and the person who we really are.

Martyr syndrome

This one makes me laugh. I'm probably the only one laughing to myself, but still, I find it ridiculous and by commenting on this I'm probably going to be making some enemies. I'm ok with that – it's their loss. Plus I'm only an enemy in their mind, I want nothing but good things for these people.

Some people in this line of work really consider themselves to be mavericks, that they are fighting for what's right, and they believe they are going against the grain in the name of good. Some people go as far as to think self-sacrificing is somewhat honourable as it either 'proves' how much they want to be a psychologist or how dedicated they are to helping others. One of my colleagues called me 'Iron Lady' once, but she probably saw me as someone who was cold hearted, living in my high tower stealing milk from children. Well, perhaps I seem blunt at times. That's mostly because I feel certain in what I want and I want other people to achieve that sense of certainty and security. The thing is, I have so much respect for this colleague – she is brilliant, incredibly intelligent, and thoughtful. I believe she is doing excellent work and I sincerely wish her all the best in her future endeavours. Her perception of me is based on the premise that she sees herself as somewhat of a maverick, a martyr, going to the ends of the earth for what she thinks is right. She will write and re-write letters, posts, and blogs in the hope that she will get other people's attention and that the 'seniors in their high towers' will respond. But yet she hates the people who she perceives are hierarchical and in power.

As brilliant as she is, she is pretty bad at implementing basic psychology in real life. You can't make people genuinely change, do what you want, or even listen to you by going against them and insulting them. You have to engage them in real conversations, you have to understand their perspective and empathise with them. Formulate them, recognise their experiences, and what would be most helpful for them. These people have problems and goals too you know and the only way we can move forward is if we work together to win together. Not by writing in some small forum that no one is listening to. Don't get me wrong, words are powerful and it is important to express oneself. But what she is doing is not going to make any real change. If nothing else, it is an illusion that she is working hard 'fighting the man'. You need to step out of this mentality and identify something helpful and meaningful, that can impact people on a large scale. People who know me on a personal level know that I am an investor and have a property portfolio. Every time I make a profit, I donate anonymously to a specific orphanage I'm familiar with in Africa. Up till now, I've donated the amount of 6-figures. With the currency conversion rates, you can imagine how this money has helped provide food, clean water, shelter, medical care, and education for these kids. I'm not saying this to brag at all, I'm actually quite private about this. I'm only saying this to demonstrate a point – this is real change. Not some random letter that gets posted straight into the trash. If you really want to make real change, figure out a way that is not simply an outlet for your frustrations. And if you can't work out a way, feel free to contact me – I'm more than willing to think this through with anyone who is serious about making helpful changes.

One way traffic

Throughout this career path, there will be several moments when you feel there is a one way traffic system in place. You will feel as though the tutors, supervisors, and managers will dominate all. Whatever they say goes. You have no voice, you have no importance, and you are devalued. Very sadly this can transpire in many ways. I would recommend you read the book Man's Search for Meaning by Victor Frankl. Inspiring neurologist and psychiatrist lived through World War 2 and experienced the devastating impact it had on humanity. Remarkably he held onto his personal strength and resilience which helped him survive. This book is so insightful and provides so much meaning to humanity and can provide us with lessons to help us through life, as well as how we navigate this world of becoming a psychologist where we feel powerless to the powers that be.

Other people cannot destroy you if you do not give them power to do so. The more connected you are to other people and the more you provide them with the sense of hierarchy, control, and dominance, the more they will own it in reality and / or in your mind. This therefore naturally puts you in a position whereby you have no other choice but to be powerless, helpless, and submissive. Whether you take this position willingly or resisting it, you are taking this position by the very action of acknowledging their power and superiority.

At the start of the clinical training course, I was mindful of this power imbalance and I was somewhat frightened that I would be subpar, that I had to submit and nod my head to anything and everything. Other people in my course decided to rebel and speak out when they felt there was injustice occurring but that only fed into this power imbalance. They were speaking out against those in power, thus acknowledging the course had 'the power' and they did not. I took a different approach. Not an approach accepted by a lot of other people but man I tell you it was an approach that worked wonders. I stopped giving a f*ck. Well and truly, couldn't give any f*cks about the course. I was there, I turned up, did what I needed to do, but that was it. I didn't need to invest emotionally into this. I recognised I was a human being as much as anyone else there including the other trainees and tutors, and that's all it needed to be. The course was not a magical and powerful entity. It was just something constructed by a bunch of people who did the best they could for what they knew at that time. Let me tell you though the less of a f*ck I gave, the better my experience was. I did well in my placements passing all sections, my assignments all passed without requiring any corrections, and my exam results substantially improved. Not only this, my mental wellbeing improved. I went on holiday at least 6 times a year and I did what I was meant to do: live life. Not live the course. Please, get over yourself, the course ain't all that and why would I make it so? Save your f*cks for what you care about and what is meaningful to you and your life.

Principle 42

"Accept everything about yourself, I mean everything. You are you and that is the beginning and the end. No apologies, no regrets", Clark Moustakas.

Principle 43

"The art of being yourself at your best is the art of unfolding yourself into the personality you want to be. Learn to love yourself, be gentle with yourself, to forgive yourself, for only as we have the right attitude toward ourselves can we have the right attitude towards others", Wilfred Peterson.

Principle 44

""Rest and self-care are so important. When you take time to replenish your spirit, it allows you to serve others from the overflow. You cannot serve from an empty vessel", Eleanor Brownn.

Principle 45

"Remember, you have been criticising yourself for years and it hasn't worked. Try approving of yourself and see what happens", Louise Hay.

CHAPTER 22
Care to listen? Food for thought for institutions

I have spent a lot of time and energy discussing the difficulties of becoming a clinical psychologist from the perspective of the individuals attempting to pursue this career – the university students, assistant psychologists, and trainee clinical psychologists. I hope that *if* anyone reading this happens to be a placement clinical supervisor or represents the university as a clinical tutor, academic tutor, or academic director, they would put their busy schedules on hold to empathise with those who are working to becoming clinical psychologists. But alas, often one is the centre of one's universe and they have other goals in mind. More often than not, they may struggle to appreciate the heartache that people go through. Supervisors, tutors, or institutions may not only neglect to provide support for those who are developing their career but rather add to their pain by demanding more and more.

In the hope of supporting all individuals, I have spent time considering what supervisors, tutors, and institutions would have to hear so they can understand what people like me go through. I hope that this would encourage them to take time to reflect upon their practices and how they could make the process better. I may not have all the answers for what should happen to change and improve the system, but I do know that what is now is not enough. Institutions and supervisors always request feedback from students; however the feedback is rendered meaningless as it appears they struggle to hear what the student or trainee is saying. I urge tutors, supervisors, and institutions to permit themselves to understand students, assistant psychologists, and trainee clinical psychologists – we are all human and all have something to share within this process. But this is the key problem: institutions and people involved within do not permit themselves to understand in order to change. They listen with the intention of response, rather than listening with the intention of understanding. I hope you can think about the following quote by Carl Rogers and how it is necessary to allow ourselves to understand others. "I have found it of enormous value when I can permit myself to understand the other person. The way in which I have worded this statement may seem strange to you. Is it necessary to permit oneself to understand another? I think it is. Our first reaction to most of the statements which we hear from other people is an evaluation or judgement, rather than an understanding of it... Very rarely do we permit ourselves to understand precisely what the meaning of the statement to the other person." Often institutions listen to concerns raised by individuals with the intention to provide a response, rather than the intention to understand. It is only through institutions understanding what students, assistants, and trainees mean that helpful change can occur in order to facilitate future development of the profession.

This chapter discusses themes which reflect the difficult relationship between institutions governing the process of becoming a clinical psychologist and those individuals getting into the profession. I map and describe what appears to occur between institutions (including tutors, and supervisors) and people who are working towards becoming clinical psychologists. I include suggestions on ways in which institutions, tutors, and supervisors may wish to consider in order to support students, assistant psychologists, and trainees with respect to their educational development and their personal wellbeing.

The dynamics between institutions and those who aspire to be clinical psychologists

The dynamics are clear and they are difficult to navigate. Based on a lot of research and reflecting upon my own personal experiences as well as other qualifying and qualified clinical psychologists, I have formulated what happens to create such a dreadful experience. Here, I used a formulation to describe the ongoing dynamics because I thought I would use a method which clinical psychologists (institutions and aspiring) would generally understand. For ease, I have used the label 'institutions' to encompass universities that governs training for clinical psychologists, as well as clinical tutors, supervisors, academic tutors, and course directors who represent the process of getting onto the clinical doctorate training. I have used the label 'aspiring clinical psychologist' to describe people who are wanting to become qualified clinical psychologists. I frequently reference to this group of individuals as trainee clinical psychologists however the themes discussed may be applicable to other people at different stages of their career, including undergraduate or postgraduate students and assistant psychologists. A final note, you may criticise this map for not being based on a specific theory or that the themes identified were not developed through strict qualitative analysis. However, the themes described have transpired over the years and are evident through objective observation and personal reports. The direction of flow reflects how certain themes influence others.

Map 1. The dangerous game of power and wellbeing

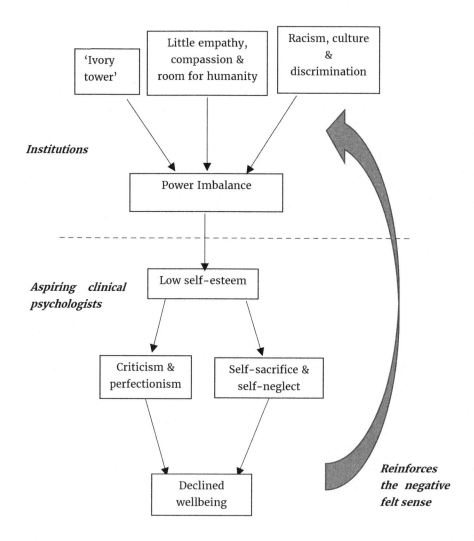

This all starts off with a very obvious inequality, as demonstrated by the dotted line, between the institutions who have the power to train someone to qualify as a clinical psychologist and people who are desperate to receive training. This inequality is inherited within the dynamics between 'training institution' and 'students', and this is something that is generally acceptable within society. Although this inequality is fact and cannot be changed, it becomes a bitter pill to swallow when unhealthy features are involved which create a difficult power imbalance. This power imbalance consequently has a negative impact on the wellbeing of aspiring clinical psychologists. We begin by discussing these unhealthy features and how they feed into the power imbalance, creating distress for aspiring clinical psychologists, and how these features maintain one another.

'Ivory tower'

Remember how I described that getting onto the clinical doctorate training is almost like trying to find Hogwarts? That it is reserved only for the 'special and the elite'? The clinical doctorate training has an 'ivory tower' aura surrounding it in two broad senses:

1. ***Provoked by the clinical doctorate training programme.*** The universities providing the clinical training as well as course directors, academics, and clinical tutors representing clinical training emit a sense of superiority. Albeit this may not be true of all universities, some suggest that the training programme, the university, or even the lecturers are somehow better than the rest. This includes other universities, disciplines, qualifications, and professions. The manner in which the university presents itself and course directors conduct themselves suggest that this training programme is first-class and it is reserved for the truly elite. Ironically, as much as subjects taught on the training programme involves an encouragement of equality, the programme itself does not embody this essence. In fact, something about the way in which the training programme is designed segregates itself from

society, distancing themselves from the 'common folk'. They do this in several ways:

a. Those representing the clinical doctorate training programme, the course directors, tutors, clinical supervisors, and research supervisors all compete to demonstrate their level of academic achievement. They all want to show everyone else that they have spent the last 125 years doing research for 25 hours a day (no, that's not a typo). They fight to achieve professorship level and whatever else obscure academic title to show that they are super clever. They even b*tch about each other on 'who got the grant this time around and did they really deserve it because I would have done a better job of it'. Frankly, all this shows is that their life is their work, to which I pity. But that's their life choice which I respect. It's simply unfortunate that individuals representing the training programme embody the very exact meaning of elites.

b. Universities often have a 'Clinical or Service User Liaison Group' which is essentially a group of individuals who provide consultation to trainees and / or researchers around important matters including what to do to support service users in certain situations, topic areas that are really relevant for service users, how would service users like to be treated etc. Having such conversations with individuals who have received treatment from services is vital to ensure that future clinical work is helpful and safe. The opinions of service users matter far more than the opinions of academics, as service users have had real–life experiences whilst academics have the experience of burying their noses in dusty books. However, when course directors recommend trainees to contact this service user group, they do it because they are obliged to under ethical regulations and policies, not because they want to. Unfortunately, it often appears that course directors and / or other individuals representing the training programme have a disdain for the service user liaison group. They resent some of the recommendations made and frequently 'tactfully amend' the recommendation to fit in with their view of what 'should' happen. Is this respecting service users or simply a paperwork exercise followed by manipulation? At the end of it all, the service user liaison group barely have a say in the training programme and often face the 'ivory tower', segregated from the 'intelligent academics', despite being requested to be involved in the university and its training.

c. The way in which trainees are treated by those representing the training programme may differ dependent upon their previous qualifications, their social class, the way they talk, the way they dress, their race, and their apparent financial state. Trainees who appear to have come from working class backgrounds or who may wear cheap and torn clothes (no, not trendy torn jeans) may be subtly looked down upon and negatively evaluated. This can be reflected in their results for spoken exams or presentations, as well as simple class discussions.

d. Access to the training programme is designed in such a way that can feel unfair. Individuals who may not know the 'right' thing to say on their application form, or who do not have previously graduated from prestigious universities or worked at reputable NHS Trusts may be viewed negatively. Some training programmes heavily rely on your references; having referees that are well known and provide a great reference goes in your favour more than an unknown referee with an excellent reference. Unfortunately, people cannot choose 'who writes their reference' as their choices are limited to the reality of their work. But again, this is another example of favouring those who are attached to notable professionals rather than people who may be equally worthy who are associated with unknown professionals.

2. *Promoted by trainees:* The second category emanates from trainees of the clinical doctorate programme, though in actual fact it is caused by the training programme itself. Individuals who are

accepted onto the clinical doctorate training course lavish in the sense that they are 'special' as they have been selected out of hundreds and hundreds of other people. Their ego gets a boost either by themselves or by other people. After years of being told that there is a good chance they will never succeed, they have 'factual evidence' that they are indeed 'better than the rest'. It's nice to feel that way, especially given the many states of hopelessness people tend to experience before they are offered a place. Whether it be deliberate or inadvertent, these individuals are then viewed by other people including peers and ex-colleagues (such as other assistant psychologists) as superior. They are seen to have succeeded in finding their place at the top of the golden tower, considered worthy by the 'powerful elders' of the clinical doctorate training programme. These people have been welcomed into the ivory tower, leaving the rest of people behind.

Racism, culture, & discrimination

I remember one lecturer said to us "if you notice, the people who work in this building 9-5 are white and middle class, but the people who work 7-9am or 5-8pm are of an ethnic minority". This in itself illustrates the power of race and discrimination. It's sad really, given we're in the 21st Century and after the recent Black Lives Matters campaigns, I thought we'd progress from such issues, but alas here we are.

Issues around race and discrimination transpires across many facets of the clinical doctorate training programme.

- *People who represent the clinical doctorate training programme*: I hate saying this, but this is what I have beard witness to: most people who represent the training programme are Caucasian and middle- or upper-class. And remember that Clinical or Service User Liaison group I mentioned earlier? Many of those individuals are from an ethnic minority. Perhaps this symbolises what occurs in society at large; people from an ethnic minority background are generally given fewer opportunities to succeed, they are more likely to become socially deprived, they are vulnerable to many prejudices and consequential abuses. Such factors increase the risk of mental health problems as well as reduce the possibility of prospering. If this is the case, why would people of ethnic minorities represent such a 'prestigious' line of work such as the clinical doctorate training programme? They wouldn't... and this is supported by universities.

"But race has nothing to do with it...": Yes, some people may argue that "it's only people with the right qualifications that would get the job" related to the clinical doctorate training programme (believe me, I can hear the course director screaming this out now). This is a valid point, in that the individual should be qualified to do their job. Employing someone who is not qualified or who is incompetent could be detrimental to themselves as they may feel overwhelmed and it could negatively impact the learning of trainees. But I do ask this: how valued are the people who represent the Clinical or Service User Liaison Group? I am particularly referring to those who are of ethnic minorities. Do they get paid at the same rate as lecturers? Do their experiences of living with mental health problems and receiving treatment mean nothing? Do their reflections of what would actually benefit services with respect to their treatment mean less than what a textbook said back in the 1900s, when which discrimination was common practice? Sadly, these individuals do not get as much 'air-time' as academic and clinical tutors do. Although I don't know for certain, it feels as though service users or people who have had experiences of mental health problems and accessing services are discriminated from providing as many lectures as they might not be 'intelligent' enough. This is incredibly shameful and disappointing. Ideally, any lecture delivered should be co-produced with a service user. That is when it is most meaningful, from both a theoretical stance as well as a humanistic real-life stance. This can and should be done if you genuinely want progression of mental health practices.

- ***Do as we say, but we don't say too much:*** There will be lectures that discuss the issue of race, culture, and socio-economic status along with associated inequalities, prejudices, and discrimination. However, these lectures are often taught by Caucasian middle-class people. Is it me or is this paradoxical and just plain stupid? It's like me saying I'm going to teach you Mandarin despite the fact I am not Chinese, I have never spoken a word of the language, and never been to China. It doesn't make much sense does it. But here we are. So do as what the lecturer thinks is the right thing to say and do when it comes to working with people of a different background, even if this isn't based on a lot. Even with such lectures that are taught with tragic irony, there is very little content that is actually meaningful. Is this perhaps because they haven't directly experienced racism or prejudice? Just something to think about...

- ***Male professors, female subordinates:*** Despite most clinical psychologists who work in academic and / or clinical settings are female, they are rarely ever at the top of the career ladder. You will find that the very few male clinical psychologists comprise most professor titles, while female clinical psychologists are... well 'just' clinical psychologists. Why? Well, the profession inherited sexism as can be seen in Freudian, Jungian, and Rogerian times and those dominating this profession are clinging on to an unhealthy history. Men who enter this profession are given a free pass to use the elevator to get to the top, while the women have to take the stairs. It's been about 8397 steps I've climbed and my legs hurt, but still haven't got to the top. The staircase never seems to end, just like a Stairmaster at the gym. You just keep climbing, knowing that you are just rotating and will always remain stationary. Another reason for this divide between male and female clinical psychologists is down to their desire to have a family. Ah yes, that old chestnut. Evidently, deciding to have a family, go on maternity leave, and spending time with loved ones ultimately means that females in this profession are neglected and ignored given their 'absence' from work. Females who do progress in this profession often either do not have a family or a partner, or they might have a family but rarely spends time with them. These women sadly sacrifice their family, becoming an inconsistent or absent parent figure to their children as they pursue their career. As much as these women may adore their children or partner and want to spend time with them, they are strongly pressured and discouraged to do so in the hope that they might be recognised by their male peers. These women spend all day and night working, above and beyond their contracted hours. Where is the choice in this? Where is the equality? Does womb = unable to progress? And I speak to my male colleagues – where are you supporting your female co-workers? Where is your respect and admiration for their work, efforts, and success? Give credit where credit is due. Rather than ignoring your female colleague for being absent at work (particularly when it is out of hours) because she is spending time with her family, how about checking in with her and seeing if there is anything she needs? When you route for each other, you grow together and success is inevitable.

Little empathy, compassion, & room for humanity

This issue revolves around how the university and representing course directors, tutors, and supervisors behave towards trainees. Many of the issues here relate to themes described in previous chapters around expectation of relentless working as well as perfectionistic standards required by the clinical doctorate training programme. The overall essence is that "you must work and work is what you must do; there is little room for being human here". Over the years, I have witnessed many trainees have their wellbeing including their physical welfare and emotional needs neglected, if not pushed to their extremity, throughout their time training. This can occur in so many aspects.

- *Physical illnesses*: if you are physically unwell and require time off from university lectures or clinical placement, you are frequently met with interrogation alongside hostility. In all fairness, the university's 'sick policy' reflects that of the NHS which is not great anyway. More than three incidents of sick leave in one year calls for an HR review followed by a monitoring period. Further incidents of sick leave can lead to further investigations and you are called into questioning, along with your reputation and work ethic. Trainees keep pushing through any bit of ill-health to avoid such negative judgement and to demonstrate that they are genuinely working hard. Unfortunately, this only leaves them to feel more rundown as they have little time to recuperate, eventually leading to further sickness that could last for a longer time or be more severe. Do you (providers of the clinical training programme) think people who have worked insanely hard to get to this stage take sick leave for fun or just to have a bit of time to 'relax'? No. People who get to the stage of training have almost killed themselves working to get here. They value their work and have a strong work ethic. They have fallen sick because they have worked too hard, not too little. Don't appear to 'punish' those who have taken time off because their body could not keep them going. Provide support to ensure that they are healed and they are cared for. If trainees do not have their health, they have nothing. They will not develop professionally, the training programme will not have trained anyone, the NHS will be understaffed, and service users ultimately suffer. To the training programme I would say make sure you have ordered your priorities correctly. There should be less emphasis on the 'three sicknesses and you are investigated' and more emphasis on physical wellbeing. This should be instilled and modelled during training and to assistant psychologists because this attitude of 'work till you die' still haunts qualified clinical psychologists who struggle to prioritise and care for their physical health.

- ***Disabilities and other special needs***: I hope this is an area that has improved but I'm not sure. I have come across several trainees who have disabilities, visible and non-visible, and unfortunately there are very little adaptations made for them. Reasons for the lack of adaptations often tend to be pathetic excuses e.g. "we need to order x equipment" or "we're waiting on funding for x" or "the elevator is broken so... sit in the café and get feedback from other trainees about the lecture afterwards". How about working with the individual to identify what is the fastest and most appropriate solution to help them feel as comfortable as possible and be directed by them as to what they need and how you could best meet this? Just because someone's disability is not visible doesn't make it non-existent. They're arguably struggling more as they receive less acknowledgement and thus less support around their needs. Be mindful of what people need and how to help them. Surely this is the entire essence of what healthcare and clinical psychology is all about.

- ***Emotional & mental wellbeing***. Well this one has gone out of the window. Why ensure that trainees are emotionally and mentally well? We should just assume that they are right? As mentioned in chapter 21, many training courses rarely advocate trainees have 'emotional wellbeing days'. Training programmes may tell trainees that they should engage in self-care but it is unclear what this actually looks like – remember trainees are looking up to you for wisdom and knowledge. Model what self-care looks like, talk to them about how self-care should make them feel, and how they should do it consistently so that they are functioning their best. Many people leave training knowing there is a thing called self-care but rarely understand or experience it fully. Furthermore, how can trainees engage in self-care if they are asked to work relentlessly? It is not even feasible. There is simply not enough time allocated for this and whatever spare time there is, trainees are probably catching up on sleep. Conversations about how the training programme, expectations, pressures, exams, assignments, placements, and workload affects trainee's wellbeing is rarely discussed. There is often little acknowledgement that life actually happens outside of the training programme, that people experience bereavements, relationship breakdowns, and changes in life circumstance, all of which can affect their emotional wellbeing. Trainees are often scrutinised and penalised for taking time off work due to emotional distress, despite the profession at large understanding that people in society are unable to function or go to work due to emotional distress. Another pinnacle of irony; a profession that aims to support people's emotional wellbeing and mental health become incapable of supporting their own emotional wellbeing. The trainee's ability to self-care and maintain their personal mental health is stunted by the course itself. Tragic. Because such irony is apparently not enough, many clinical doctorate training courses do not promote personal therapy for trainees: we provide therapy to other people, never to receive it. Receiving personal therapy is not necessarily taboo but it is not welcomed with open arms either. As much as the training programme indorses the banishment of stigma around therapy, there is an awkward sense when a trainee openly discloses that they have been receiving therapy. The list of issues around the neglect of trainee's emotional wellbeing is endless and it I am frustrated that I even have to explain the multiple levels of irony or ridiculousness that is attached to this. But I hope that course directors and institutions recognise the importance of staff mental health.

- **Bad supervisors & bad placements:** The majority of individuals who go onto the clinical doctorate training course have had their fair share of supervisors who are either incompetent, abusive, critical, or absent, as well as placements that have been stressful, overwhelming, unmanageable, and draining. Trainees may voice such concerns to the university with the hope of seeking guidance and a solution to their worries. Trainees are hopeful that their concerns would be met with compassion, empathy, and offers of practical solutions. However, like the many other things that are neglected on this training programme, so are such concerns. The trainee's university clinical tutor may provide a supportive listening ear depending on their relationship, but often little can be physically done to improve the situation. It's a tough situation in all fairness as the university may have a limited number of work placements or supervisors to draw upon and so everyone would have to 'put up' with what there is. Trainees understand this and often hope that the university clinical supervisors would be able have a discussion with the placement supervisor or recognise ways in which things can change so that we can make the best out of a bad situation. Whether or not this happens depends upon the university staff; some are fantastic in resolving this situation (see, I do give credit where credit is due), and some unfortunately do not. I am unsure why some university staff struggle to approach such situations, whether it be due to a lack of their personal confidence or conflict of interests, and perhaps this is a point for the university board to consider to ensure that university staff (clinical and academic tutors) work consistently and effectively.

Power imbalance

The issues described above feed into the difficult power imbalance experienced by the institutions and those aspiring to become clinical psychologists. If we are being completely honest, the power imbalance does not only exist between these two groups of individuals, but it also exists between male and female clinical psychologists, professionals and consulting service user groups, people of different socio-economic status and ethnic backgrounds. For the purposes of this book, I will primarily focus on the power imbalance between institutions and people who are aspiring to become clinical psychologists. Much of what I have referred to earlier in this chapter relates to trainee clinical psychologists; however this can also be seen in assistant psychologists and psychology students. A certain hierarchy is experienced, and although a real power divide exists which cannot be ignored (i.e. the institution is technically your trainer, employer, and boss), this reality is made much more painful when those who aspiring to be clinical psychologists their needs and rights are denied. This can occur across a multitude of areas:

- **Would you like cynicism with that criticism sir?** Like I've noted time and again throughout this book, criticism is the rule, not the exception. Institutions and those representing universities appear to become accustomed to the idea of negative criticism, that this is normal and should be expected in any area of oneself. It also appears that institutions are surprised when those who are criticised get upset – it is as if getting upset at critical statements is abnormal. Criticism occurs in all facets, just to name a few:

    o *Exams*: No matter how well you perform in exams, criticism will always accompany your grade. It makes sense that any exam paper would be marked with comments by which people can make improvements; however, there are rarely comments indicating what the person has done well to achieve their grade. The way in which the marking system is means that the person is lost, unaware of what they have done correctly and what 'stuff' they should keep. This is tricky because it could potentially leave the person performing worse in future exams as they begin to focus on other areas (to which are criticised) and lose their initial strengths. What would it be like for examiners to make some fair comments on both sides of the fence? The good and the bad?

    o *Assignments*. There is always room for improvement and people who aspire to be clinical psychologists understand this and do wish to better themselves. But again, like exams many of the comments are often critical and little mention is made of what the person has excelled at. As indicated by social learning theory, negative reinforcement and punishment rarely works; the best way a person can learn is by praising them of what they have done well and praise their intention to improve on other areas. Maybe something for the training programme to consider?

o   *Wellbeing*. This encompasses both the physical and emotional wellbeing of people who aspire to be clinical psychologists. As noted before, when one attempts to care for themselves, scrutiny often follows as there is a sense by the institution that they "don't believe" you were unwell. Again, this feeds into the experience of criticism, and amplifies the power imbalance with respect to who is and who is not allowed to prioritise their wellbeing.

-   ***Suggestions for lectures***. Trainees are asked to provide feedback around lectures they attend. This process on the surface appears helpful as improvements can then be made to enhance learning. Unfortunately though this feedback request often happens at the end of the lecture and at this point the lecture cannot be replaced, thus improvements upon such learning is lost. At times, trainees may provide suggestions for lecture content and feedback at the start or during the lecture. This would be incredibly helpful if the lecturer is able to hear (aka understand) the feedback and what is wanted in order to meet the trainee's needs. Sadly, this may not many happen as the lecture slides have already been written and many tutors stick to the style of death by PowerPoint. This may only seem like a small thing but in fact it illustrates another facet of power imbalance; the training provided does not match what is needed by those who are being trained. The training provided matches what the trainers think is important because, well, they are always right.

-   ***Trainees seeking discussions around exam or assignment results***. Many trainees may wish to gain further feedback and explanations around why they received the grade that they did for their exams and / or assignments. This is because they feel that the points of criticism noted in their feedback is insufficient or unexplanatory and therefore wish to understand exactly how they could improve. Some trainees may also seek such discussion so that they can gain a bit of praise around areas in which they have performed well, you know, because they never receive praise. Sadly, trainees who seek such a conversation from university tutors are frequently met with blunt and / or brief responses that basically repeat the written feedback. Trainees can read, that's not the problem. They just want further understanding and empathy to be shown by tutors, in that perhaps the tutors wish to understand the trainee's perspective. But no, there is little need from the university to develop a shared understanding with the trainee. This exemplifies another power imbalance struggle.

- ***Year group feedback.*** Every so often, trainees are invited to congregate with clinical training course tutors to discuss their perspectives of particular lectures, assignments, exams, structure of the training and placements. This is a good idea in principle. In principle, such feedback from trainees should be understood by the course and considered to amend and improve the training programme. However, this principle falls flat on its face when course directors listen to trainee's feedback with the intention to respond and defend themselves rather than with the intention to understand and action. This defensive response and maintenance of what institutions have traditionally held as 'best practice' ignores the core principle we see in every other aspect of society – things change over time in order to improve upon the past. But maintaining the stance of resistance and the ability to do so by the institution is symbolic of their power; they can do anything they think is appropriate. The power divide is again evident. So why ask trainees for feedback? Is it a mere paper exercise to demonstrate good will? I'm too busy checking my make-up in the mirror to engage in this.

Low self-esteem

As you can imagine, the never-ending criticism and neglect by the institutions leaves those who aspire to be clinical psychologists feeling worthless, anxious, and depressed. I have known several people who have aspired to be clinical psychologists and sadly, due to the nature of the game, they have sought psychopharmacological treatment (medication to treat their anxiety and depression). It is really sad that this is the result of the clinical training course and the consequential effects on the trainee's self-esteem. As much as I primarily reference the effects of the clinical training course upon trainees, the entire system of how one becomes a clinical psychologist has a detrimental impact on those who aspire to get into the profession, including students and assistant psychologists. In a competitive world where you are nothing but criticised and scrutinised, how could that not affect your self-esteem or self-worth.

Criticism & perfectionism

What one learns, one becomes. When someone has been criticised repeatedly throughout their profession, a part of their inner self integrates this voice and they too begin to criticise themselves. They therefore become the criticiser and they are the one who also hears that criticism. They become trapped in their own voice of criticism and cannot escape. I have to say, out of absolutely everything *I really mean everything* I learnt throughout my career journey, my biggest lesson was how to criticise myself endlessly. Despite receiving many bouts of therapy, it's so hard to quieten down that voice of criticism or to enhance a voice of self-compassion when I genuinely struggle to connect to it or believe that I am worthy of experiencing kindness. The aim of anything I do is perfection, and if it is not perfect it is essentially garbage. If I am not first, I have lost. In the pursuit of perfection, I constantly feel inadequate, I am never good enough and I can never be good enough no matter how much I try. And I know I am not alone in this. The reason we feel this way is because we rarely received kindness. It is only since I have qualified and had a compassionate supervisor that I have been able to hold the voice of compassion in mind (albeit not for long), but it is definitely a step in the right direction. If institutions and those representing institutions who provide the clinical doctorate training programme showed compassion towards those aspiring to qualify as clinical psychologists, the wellbeing of professionals in the system would be much better.

Self-sacrifice & self-neglect

Given how much people strive working towards becoming clinical psychologists, other areas of their life suffer as a consequence. They provide the profession all of their time and energy, which they will never get back. These people sacrifice time with their family and friends, hobbies, leisure activities, taking care of their body and mind, as well as self-care in the hope that spending more time at the office will help them get recognised. A part of them believes that the sacrifice of their lives, personal wellness, and physical and emotional health will eventually lead them to the right path of the profession. Unfortunately, this sacrifice simply results in their mind, body, and soul to be neglected. The time and energy they spend on developing their career is something they will never get back. Time is the only currency that is constantly spent and never retrieved. Losing time with your loved ones as well as experiences that feed your spirit is a real tragedy as that is something you can never get back, and before you know it, it would be too late as relationships disintegrate, places and people change, and your priority to work strengthens. As noted by the great George Bernard Shaw, "there are two tragedies in life. One is to lose your heart's desire. The other is to gain it". This demonstrates that although individuals may gain their desire of progressing through the profession, they certainly lose their heart's desire of having a fulfilled and joyful life as they sacrifice and neglect themselves for their profession. And this is the gift that the projection of the profession gives you.

Declined wellbeing

Facing discrimination, external criticism, and a power imbalance as well as experiencing a combination of self-neglect, self-criticism, and low self-esteem would undoubtably leave the individual feeling horrific. This would affect both their body and mind. How could it not affect them? The individual constantly experiences nightmares in their mind and negative voices that are always chattering away. Their personal psychological and emotional wellbeing would naturally decline. Not only this, their physical health would get neglected as they rush to eat quick take away meals and skip the gym, all so that they can spend those extra precious moments to work. This in itself would leave the person feeling unhealthy.

There are other reasons as to why one's psychological and physical wellbeing would decline. The link between the mind and body is generally common knowledge; when one goes wrong the other soon follows, and when one goes right the other improves too. When experiencing emotional distress, certain stress hormones are released including adrenaline, noradrenaline, and cortisol, which can affect one's immune system, blood pressure, and sleep patterns. Such effects on the body can have a negative impact upon one's physical health and make the person much more susceptible to illnesses. The individual feels drained and is unable to engage in their normal daily activities. Feeling physically unhealthy and hormonal changes including an increase of stress hormones and a reduction of pleasure hormones can mean that the person is more prone to developing depression and / or anxiety. And so the two sided problem perpetuates one another; one's psychological and physical wellbeing both decline.

The other, and perhaps less thought about, problem around those who aspire to be clinical psychologists feeling deflated is that it creates a level of sensitivity to further negative comments or negative experiences from institutions. Individuals may expect difficulty to a certain extent; however, being constantly criticised and neglected can often mean that they become hypersensitive to further criticism and neglect. They are also more likely to negatively interpret situations that are 'ambiguous' or that do not have an objective negative meaning. This suggests that even when institutions do not intend to be so negative towards those who aspire to be clinical psychologists, they may appear to be negative and punitive anyway, which reinforces the negative felt sense of all the themes described above. This in itself perpetuates the negative vicious cycle. For institutions to be perceived as kind, they need to act in such a way to break such a cycle.

Where does that leave us?

"Love is the supreme form of communication. In the hierarchy of needs, love stands as the supreme developing agent of the humanity of the person. As such, the teaching of love should be the central core of all early childhood curriculum with all other subjects growing naturally out of such teaching", Abraham Maslow.

For decades, research has demonstrated time and again that learning can occur in different formats, but ultimately for effective learning to occur the individual must feel safe, soothed, and loved. The institutions that provide clinical training sadly fail to create such an environment as the system causes a sense of fear, anxiety, and hopelessness. How could we then expect 'effective' learning to occur? I have to say, as much as the clinical doctorate training programme was insanely difficult to pass; my real learning of clinical work properly started after I qualified. My guess is that many other people in my shoes had the same experience. As Maslow indicates, any subject taught should emanate out of compassion and love. This is not exclusively for children but is also applicable for adults. The 'harshness' of the system does not necessarily create 'resilience and strength' but can simply create desperation, hopelessness, and hatred. Bottom line: you don't want to create a cohort of clinicians who should be showing compassion to their patients but are unable to actually practice this towards themselves.

I've noted some points below that could support teaching. These reflect both the attitude and style of teaching that are important to embrace to (1) support effective learning and (2) reduce the likelihood that trainees will become distressed.

- **Modelling**: Modelling is the idea that teaching best occurs when the 'teacher' does what they want their 'student' to learn. Other people learn by observation and then enact what they have just witnessed. And guess what, if you model criticism, you're going to have a bunch of students who excel at it. If however you model compassion and self-care, your students are going to become more emotionally stable. Ideally, you want clinical psychologists to be emotionally stable themselves, right? So, what to model:

  o *Self-care*. What does this actually mean? What does this look like? Can we be more flexible in what 'self-care' looks like? Sometimes it may mean taking a day off work, sometimes it may mean engorging on 3 burgers.

  o *Wellbeing*. What are the different facets of wellbeing? What does wellbeing actually mean? And how do we look after it? If wellbeing relates to our psychological, emotional, mental, and physical health, then how do we take better care of all of this? If we feel able to take care of our wellbeing and we feel stable, only then we have enough strength to support others (e.g. patients) to take care of their wellbeing. Therefore, how do we model healthy wellbeing for ourselves and then for others?

  o *Compassion*. I mean this towards ourselves and others. Considering the training programme wishes for trainees to develop and improve their skills, why not do this through the voice of compassion and kindness rather than the voice of criticism and punishment? Again, if trainees are able to witness and experience compassion, it is much easier to implement towards themselves and others.

- **Positive reinforcement vs. negative reinforcement or punishment**. This is based on Social Learning Theory developed by Albert Bandura in 1977. As previously noted, this is based on the premise that people learn much more effectively if they are praised for the things that they do well, strengthening their skills, rather than criticising them for what they have done poorly. For areas which require improvement, effective learning only happens through positively enforcing actions or behaviours that are desired. A real life example may mean here are sweets as a reward for taking part in this role play exercise of delivering a specific therapy. Criticising (or even punishing) the student for getting things less than ideal actually makes them regress and potentially perform worse next time. So, how much would it really cost institution to reward trainees in order to enhance performance rather than criticising which could impair performance? Not only would positively reinforcing methods help learning, this would also improve the emotional wellbeing of trainees as they are able to identify personal strengths, recognising that they have developed skills and can master a domain of their learning.

- **Person-centred**. Services and institutions always talk about how treatment should be person-centred, it should be based specifically on the person's needs and goals, accounting for their abilities (or disabilities), cultural background, and socio-economic status. It would be really helpful if that elements of the training programme are tailored to person-centred needs of the trainee. A lot of elements taught will cover a broad range of topics (and so it should) and therefore some course directors may argue that the training programme cannot be 'person-centred' for trainees; however I would argue that you could. This could be facilitated in many aspects. For instance, we have already identified that discrimination and prejudice occurs within the profession of clinical psychology; so what would it be like to recognise trainee's differences and strive for equality to ensure fair opportunities? It would be important if university tutors spent time getting to know the trainees (given there are so few) and strive understand their personal circumstances, cultural backgrounds, skills, and areas of interest to support their work. People with disabilities, whether that be visible or invisible, should have their needs met with whatever it is that they require to support their wellbeing while training. Given trainees are requested to 'teach' certain topics, why not request trainees to discuss certain areas that are specific to their area of real-life knowledge? And finally, as human beings we are all unique with specific needs and desires, thus it would be important for the institution and tutors to support the trainee's needs in order to preserve their optimal personhood and wellbeing.

- **Research & therapy.** Trainees are bombarded with research statistics, methodologies, and other technical analyses when learning about something that is supposedly 'therapeutic'. Yes it is vital that trainees are learning about therapy that has been evidenced through good quality research. However, the problem is that much of the research referred to has been outdated and may become less and less relevant to what is seen in current clinical practice. Therefore, it is important that:

  o *Research is current.* By this, that we are not referring to research that is almost 50 years old but actually research completed in the past 10 years, including reviews of many studies which helps us consolidate a larger pool of evidence.

  o *Research is relevant.* That the research conducted is actually relevant to the clinical population that clinical psychologists work with. For instance, centuries ago mental health services typically believed that people accessing treatment just had the 'one' mental health problem, whereas we actually know now that having multiple mental health problems at any one time is common and perhaps the norm, not the exception. Therefore, this means that with research that evidences a therapeutic approach, it is important that the research is completed with people who would be 'typical' to access services. This also means there is perhaps less emphasis on research conducted on a normal student population, simply because you couldn't get ethics to approve of your research in the NHS...

- o *Real life experiences.* Please, please, please, have more involvement of Clinical or Service User Liaison Groups. Have people who have accessed services and have received treatment provide lectures, explaining their experiences, what was important, what was irrelevant, what was most meaningful, and how could clinicians improve. Having service user involvement in teaching is vital and it is of equal importance compared with the technical, clinical, and research element of the training programme. Hearing service user's experiences of treatment is real life evidence and it is what research is all about, thus should be involved in the teaching element of the programme. Service users should be provided priority involvement in all teaching, include them within the design of the training programme as well as each lecture provided. Have service users assessing OSCE (observed structured clinical examination) completed by trainees so that they are able to provide true feedback from a service user perspective. Having more service user involvement would make training really meaningful and insightful for trainees.

CHAPTER 23

Now you've qualified... and no-one cares ["What was the point in all this again?"]

Well, eventually after the never ending journey of trying to become a clinical psychologist, there will come a day when you actually qualify. After passing your viva, with whatever corrections you may need to do, you will be able to register your name on the HCPC as a fully-fledged qualified practicing clinical psychologist. When I got to the stage of qualifying, I thought it would be magical, envisaging fireworks going off all just for me in celebration of my efforts to get to this stage. But alas, it's not quite that fancy. The best you could hope for is to have a £2 drink bought for you by the course directors. Well, at least you can breathe a sigh of relief as you are now considered 'good enough' to be a clinical psychologist. With this, you will be going out into the big wide world of clinical and / or research work.

As much as there was a constant narrative around being humble, working within your zone of competency, seeking guidance from your supervisor, you are now set free and expected to be fully competent. You can no longer rely on writing "under the supervision of [supervisor's name]" to protect yourself or your work. It's astonishing how you can be controlled for so long, receive the message that your work is inadequate and then suddenly be expected to feel comfortable and confident with your work. Not to worry though, the journey you have been on has been tough and it is designed in such a way that you would develop appropriate competency unconsciously. As supervision, guidance, and evidence based practice is embraced by all clinical psychologists at large, you will always be able to access some form of support from others in the field. Thus you continue your development and learning after qualifying. If anything, I felt as though my real learning came after qualifying (sorry to scare you if I have). It's kind of like learning how to drive – you learn the theory and manoeuvres but you only really learn how to drive in a competent and confident way after you pass your test and you have to drive alone. The surprising thing is that more often than not other professionals do not tend to care that much about you being a qualified clinical psychologist. Colleagues who do not really understand the difference between qualified, trainee, or assistant psychologist and are willing to take recommendations from anyone 'psychology' related. And what's more, they may not particularly care about the type of approach you are using with service users in therapeutic or research settings. If anything, you are pretty free to pick and choose as you please, and as long as you can find some kind of justification, no-one really tends question it. But please, as it should go without saying, continue to work in an ethical, person-centred, evidence-based, and compassionate way.

Final note

I hope you enjoyed reading this book. It was written with the intention to help people to become a clinical psychologist at every stage of their career journey. I believe the advice provided throughout can improve your way of working, both academically and professionally, and create better results for you. I sincerely hope this book also provides a sense of hope for those of you struggling at any point as I empathise with the tragedies that occur on this journey. Above all, I genuinely want each and every one of you to take care of your own psychological wellbeing, embrace love and kindness, and show yourself the compassion you deserve. This career path is already tough and there is no need to make it tougher, so look after yourself first and foremost. The rest will follow suit.

Printed in Great Britain
by Amazon

78629617R00112